The Art of Business Warfare

The Art of Business Warfare

Outmaneuvering Your Competition with Military Tactics

David W. Leppanen

Writers Club Press

San Jose New York Lincoln Shanghai

The Art of Business Warfare
Outmaneuvering Your Competition with Military Tactics

Writers Club Press
an imprint of iUniverse.com, Inc.

For information address:
iUniverse.com, Inc.
5220 S 16th, Ste. 200
Lincoln, NE 68512
www.iuniverse.com

ISBN: 0-595-14108-0

Printed in the United States of America

To Mom, Dad, and my sister Kim for their love, patience and support.

Contents

Acknowledgements

Thanks to the following military officers for their input:

Lt. Col. Wallace Erickson, Lt. Col. Kenneth Finlayson, Maj. William McElrath, Capt. Victoria Goodge, Capt. James Keith, Capt. Paul Nordvall, Capt. Angela Pilate

Thanks to the following businesspersons for their input: Michael Arntson, Todd Balsimo, Daniel Kantos, and Jeffrey Ruchie

Editing Dave Perry

Thanks to the librarians at:

Washington County Library System, Stillwater, Minnesota

Ramsey County Library System, St. Paul, Minnesota

1. Six Similarities between Business and Warfare

"*We are at war*"

—Dennis Long, former president of
Budweiser in a 1978 internal memo[1].

Comparing business to war is nothing new. Barrie G. James' 1984 book *Business Wargames*, applies military tactics and strategy to business. In their book, *Marketing Warfare*, Al Ries and Jack Trout write "we think the best book on marketing was written by a retired Prussian general, Karl von Clausewitz. Entitled *On War* it outlines the strategic principles behind all successful wars." In the movie *Wall Street* Gordon Gekko (Michael Douglas) gives Bud Fox (Charlie Sheen) some business advice. "Read Sun Tzu *The Art of War*. Every battle is won before it's ever fought. Think about it…its trench warfare out there, pal."

Businesses have more in common with the military than most people realize.

1. The organizational structures of the military and business are similar.

Look at the hierarchy of a corporation and compare it to that of a military organization:

Business	Military
CEO/Presidents	Generals
Vice-Presidents	Colonels/Majors
Managers	Captains
Assistant Managers	lst Lieutenants
Manager Trainees	2nd Lieutenants
Engineers/Programmers	Warrant Officers
Supervisors	Sergeants
General workers	Enlisted Personnel

Next, compare the staff structure of the military with those of business:

Business	Military
Human Resources/Accounting	Gl Personnel/Administration
Sales/Marketing	G2 Intelligence
Operations	G3 Operations
Purchasing/Shipping/Receiving	G4 Logistics

2. Both build organizations that maintain a core ideology in specific, tangible ways.

When a person enlists in the military they recite the following oath:

I, (person's name) do solemnly swear (or affirm) that I will support and defend the Constitution of the United States against all enemies, foreign and domestic; that I will bear true faith and allegiance to the same; and that I will obey the orders of the President of the United States and the orders of the officers appointed over me, according to regulations and the Uniform Code of Military Justice. So help me God.

In the mid-1980s, Sam Walton, founder of Wal-Mart had over one hundred thousand Wal-Mart employees recite the following oath during a TV satellite linkup:

Now, I want you to raise your right hand-and remember what we say at Wal-Mart, that a promise we make is a promise we keep-and I want you to repeat after me: From this day forward, I solemnly promise and declare that every time a customer comes within ten feet of me, I will smile, look him in the eye, and greet him. So help me Sam.[2]

3. Both organizations rely on teamwork to accomplish their goal.

Field Manual (FM) 22-102 *Soldier Team Development* states:

The best combat and combat support strategies and the most brilliant application of tactical operations cannot ensure victory unless soldiers in sections, squads, crews, platoons, and companies effectively perform their assigned missions. Ultimate success in the battle will depend largely on the development of cohesive combat ready teams consisting of well-trained and highly motivated soldiers.[3]

Kenneth Blanched, Ph.D., co-author of the book The *One Minute Manager Builds High Performing Teams* writes:

Never before in the history of the workplace has the concept of teamwork been more important to the functioning of successful organizations… No longer can we depend upon a few peak performers to rise to the top to lead. If we are to survive we must figure out ways to tap into the creativity and potential of people at all levels.[4]

4. Both business and the military have written guidelines governing their operations.

The designers of International Organization for Standardization (ISO) guidelines should credit the military with creating the first Good Manufacturing Practices. To assist soldiers and their units with their tasks is a vast array Army Regulations (AR), Field Manuals (FM), Technical Manuals (TM) and Standard Operating Procedures (SOP). Many businesses today utilize some form of Good Manufacturing Practices (GMP) or Total Quality Management (TQM). Many of these practices are similar to those used in the military.

5. Both have dress codes.

Many businesses have dress codes although they are not as rigid as those in the military. However, both have written guidelines—the Army has Army Regulation 670-1 *Wearing of the Uniform* and business has *John T. Malloy's Dress for Success.* A person can often tell what person's profession or position is by the way he dresses.

Disney has a strict grooming code. Men are not allowed to don facial hair. Women cannot wear heavy makeup or large dangling earrings. The dress code is strictly enforced. In 1991, members of the Disneyland staff went on strike to protest the grooming code; Disney fired the strike leader and kept the rule intact.[5]

IBM's salespersons wear conservative, white shirts, and shined shoes. When IBM first enacted its white shirt policy everyone laughed—and IBM laughed all the way to the bank.[6]

6. Both encourage physical fitness

The military has recognized that physically fit soldiers perform better in combat. The Army has developed the largest physical fitness programs in the United States and possibly in the entire world. The Soldier

Physical Fitness Center at Fort Benjamin Harrison in Indianapolis, Indiana, has become a center for physical fitness and for developing an enlightened approach to health. Programs are tailored for those in their twenties as well as those over 40. It focuses on regular exercise, good nutrition and weight control, avoiding harmful substances such as drugs and cigarettes, and learning to handle stress.

Business is also beginning to see the benefits of physical fitness. Dr. Jim Loehr and Dr. Jack Groppel have developed a corporate training program called Mentally Tough. Based at the Loehr-Groppel/Saddlebrook Science Center in Tampa Florida, the program teaches executives the principles of winning in sports as they apply to winning in business. The program stresses proper nutrition, exercise, and work habits that will allow individuals to deliver peak performance when needed.[7]

Through the years, the military has often borrowed ideas from business. Perhaps it's time for business to borrow ideas from the military. Some people argue that military principles are too rigid to be applied to today's fast changing business world. John A. Byrne, a senior writer at *Business Week* writes "…Taps is being played in corporate corridors for the whole way of doing business that was modeled on the command-and control procedures of the military."

Using former IBM CEO John F. Akers as an example, Byrne continues:

> As a 32-year IBMer, he [Akers] couldn't reinvent Big Blue swiftly enough. Chances are his successor will be younger and far more comfortable with a flatter power structure where alacrity and agility are prized over rigid, almost military, obedience.[8]

These statements warrant further examination because they are based on old methods no longer used by the military. Just as business practices evolve so does military doctrine. According FM 100-5 *Operations* the Army's success on the battlefield depends on its ability to fight in accordance with five basic tenets of the Army's Airland Battle Doctrine: initiative, agility, depth, synchronization, and versatility.

Initiative—Applied to the force, initiative is the effort to force the opponent to conform to your operational tempo while retaining your freedom of action. Applied to individual soldiers and leaders, initiative is the willingness and ability to act independently within the guidelines of the commander's intent. It also means taking prudent risks to accomplish the mission.

Agility—Agility is the ability of friendly forces to act faster than the opposition—It is the first prerequisite for seizing the initiative and permits the rapid concentration of friendly strength against enemy vulnerabilities.

Depth—Depth is the "extension of operations in space, time, and resources." It provides the commander with the needed space to maneuver; the required time to prepare and execute operations; and the critical resources to win. To think in depth is to forecast and anticipate actions so that the opposition can be attacked throughout the entire battlefield. Successful commanders realize that war is uncertain. They look beyond the requirements of the moment and forecast the actions of the future.

Synchronization—Synchronization is arranging activities in time and space to mass at the decisive point to achieve a desired effect. This means integrating such activities such as logistics, intelligence, and fire support with maneuver units maximizing the use of every available resource to insure success.

Versatility—Versatility is the ability of units to meet diverse mission requirements. Commanders must be able to shift focus, tailor forces, and move rapidly and efficiently from one mission to another. It implies an ability to be multifunctional and to operate across a full range of military operations.[9]

These military attributes are also used by businesses; they just have different names. Initiative is "empowerment" or "decentralization." Agility is "fast cycle times" or "being nimble". Depth is "forecasting," synchronization is "coordination" and versatility is "multi-skilled".

Successful companies have all these qualities. Today's companies constantly make their products obsolete before their rivals do it for them. In an attempt to becoming more responsive businesses are delegating decision making to the lowest appropriate level. In order to delegate more responsibility businesses are constantly looking for skilled people who are versatile and willing to pitch in on any jobs.

Applying military principles to business does not mean necessarily bringing death and destruction to your competitors. It does not mean relying on confrontation to achieve your goals. Sun Tzu's *The Art of War* provides advice on inflicting destruction:

1. Generally in war the best policy is to take a state intact; to ruin it is inferior to this.

2. To capture the enemy's army is better than to destroy it; to take intact a battalion, company or a five-man squad is better than to destroy them.

3. For to win one hundred victories in one hundred battles is not the acme of skill. To subdue the enemy without fighting is the acme of skill.[10]

Nor does applying military techniques require employees to snap to attention and blindly follow the instructions of their superiors. Consider this quote by General George C. Marshall on leadership:

The soldier is a man;—he expects to be treated like an adult, not a schoolboy. He has rights; they must be made known to him and thereafter respected. He has ambition; it must be stirred. He has a belief in fair play; it must be honored. He has a need for comradeship; it must be supplied. He has imagination; it must be stimulated. He has a sense of personal dignity; it must be sustained. He has pride; it can be satisfied and made the bedrock of character once he has been assured that he is playing a useful and respected role. To give a man this is the acme of inspired leadership. He has become loyal because loyalty has been given to him.[11]

William A. Cohen, author of the book *The Art of the Leader*, outlines a model of leadership called the combat model of leadership. Cohen writes:

> Combat is probably the most severe environment in which you will ever lead other human beings in accomplishing any goal. If you can apply the combat model of leadership successfully, you can be successful in leading in many difficult, but less demanding environments.[12]

Corporations such as Domino's Pizza and Honeywell send their managers to "boot camps" such as Leading Edge Boot Camps to improve their teamwork, leadership, and communication skills. Today's business environment can be compared to combat. The German military strategist Carl von Clausewitz wrote "Everything is simple in War, but the simplest thing is difficult. These difficulties accumulate and produce a friction no man can imagine exactly who has not seen in War."[13] Murphy's Law of Combat states it more bluntly. "If you are short of everything except the enemy, you are in combat."

Friction in war is equipment failures, bad weather, mistaken or incomplete intelligence, orders that are never received. Business encounters the same problems in the form of unavailable parts, production defects, excess inventory, or changes in consumer demand.

Rather than ignoring military techniques, executives should be studying the preemptive battles of eighteenth century Russian general Aleksandr Suvorov and the Israeli Army during the Six-Day War. They should be applying the dislocation techniques of the fifteenth century Bohemian squire Jan Ziska. They should be studying the disruption techniques the Germans used during their invasion of France in 1940 and General Douglas MacArthur used during the invasion of Inchon and simultaneous breakout from Pusan during the Korean War.

In their book *The Discipline of Market Leaders*, Michael Treacy and Fred Wiersema provide a case study where Airborne Express lured away some of Federal Express' accounts. Let's examine this case study from the viewpoint of a military operation. The mission: lure away the National Parts Depot, Xerox, and Luxottica accounts from FedEx. Airborne's G2 intelligence assets (Sales and Marketing) learned FedEx's strengths and weaknesses. It also studied National Parts Depot's, Xerox's, and Luxottica's requirements. It's G1 personnel/administration assets (Human Resources/Customer Service) insured that people were available to handle the new accounts. The G4 Logistics assets (Purchasing, Shipping, and Receiving) insured that distribution assets were available. The G3 Operations (Operations) coordinated the execution of service once Airborne landed the new accounts.[13]

Summary

Comparing business to war is nothing new. Successful businesses often incorporate military tactics into their corporate strategies. Businesses and the military have at least six similarities. They are:

1. **Structure.** The CEO/President duties are similar to those of a general. A manager has comparable duties to those of a captain in the Army. The responsibilities of a supervisor/foreman are similar to those of a sergeant. In business human resources/payroll/accounting would be the G1 (Personnel/Administration) in the military. Sales/marketing would be the G2 (Intelligence), Operations the G3 (Operations) and Purchasing, Shipping, and Receiving would be the G4 (Logistics).

2. Both build organizations that **maintain a core ideology** in specific, tangible ways.

3. Both rely on **teamwork**. General George S. Patton, commander of the Third Army during World War II, stated "Without this teamwork, war cannot be successfully fought."

Businesses are also realizing the importance of teamwork. In 1990, K Shoes, Ltd., a United Kingdom shoe manufacturer, began utilizing teams in its Springer plant. On time delivery has increased from 80 percent to 97 percent. Productivity per employee has risen more than 19 percent and reject rate has dropped from 5,000 parts per million to 250 per million. At Westinghouse's Electronic Assembly Plant in Texas, cycle times for many products have been reduced from twelve weeks to less than two weeks since the incorporation of teams in 1983.[15]

4. Both business and the military have **written guidelines** to govern their actions. The military uses Army Regulations, Field Manuals, Technical Manuals and Standard Operating Procedures. Businesses use International Organization Standardization and Total Quality Management Programs

5. **Dress Codes.** The Army has *AR 670-1 Wearing of the Uniform* and business has *John T. Malloy's Dress for Success.* In business you can often tell a person's profession or position by the clothes he or she is wearing.

6. **Physical fitness** is encouraged by both organizations.

2. The Principles of War

Since the first battles were fought, the principles of war have existed. Two thousand years ago, Sun Tzu, the Chinese general discussed these principles in his treatise *The Art of War*. Nineteenth century Prussian general Karl von Clausewitz wrote about the principles of war in his 1832 book *On War*. The principles of war furnish general guidelines for the execution of combat at the strategic, operational, and tactical levels. The U.S. Army published its first discussion of the principles of war in a 1921 training regulation. Listed below are the principles of war from Field Manual (FM) 100-5 *Operations* and how successful businesses have adapted them to their operations. Although each principle features a different corporation, all seven principles are usually present in successful companies.

Objective—Direct every military operation toward a clearly defined, decisive, and obtainable goal.

In war, the ultimate purpose of the military is to defeat the opposition's armed forces and destroy its will to fight. The connecting of objectives at all levels is critical; each maneuver must contribute to the strategic goal. Intermediate goals must directly, quickly, and economically contribute to the operation. Actions that do not contribute to accomplishing the objective must be avoided.

The Walt Disney Company's business is to *make people happy*. As new employees quickly learn, nobody's been hired for a job: everybody's been cast for a role in the show. Employees are "cast members." Customers are "guests." A job description is a "script" and a work shift is a "performance." To reinforce Walt Disney's concept of hospitality, the company recruits and trains every one of its employees. All employees from security officers to financial analysts must attend a Disney Tradition orientation and seminar. At Disney, it doesn't matter who the customers are, what language they speak, where they come from, or what color they are. All efforts are oriented towards making people happy.[1]

Offensive—Seize, retain, and exploit the initiative.

Offensive action is the most effective and decisive way to attain a clearly defined objective. Offensive operations allow a military force to seize and maintain the initiative while sustaining freedom of action and attaining decisive results. A defensive posture is used only as a temporary expedient and the commander must use every opportunity to seize the initiative. The force that retains the initiative through offensive engagement compels the opponent to react rather than act.

In 1985, Gillette Company's sales and profits were flat. Though highly vulnerable, Gillette managed to repulse a takeover bid form Ronald L. Perelman in 1986 and a proxy fight in 1988. When President Alfred Zeien took over in 1991, he was determined to make changes. He decreed that the Gillette must become the world leader, or have a plan to become a world leader in all of its core businesses. He also insisted that at least 50 percent of every dollar in operating profit be invested back into three growth drivers: research and development, capital expenditures, and advertising.

Gillette is now the world leader in 13 product categories, accounting for 81% of its 1996 sales—up from 50% in 1991. Since 1991, with the help from acquisitions, sales have more than doubled to $9.7 billion in 1996. It has posted 29 quarters of double—digit earnings and propelling its market value to $56 billion, 14 times what corporate raider Perleman proposed in 1986.[2]

Gillette incorporates a strategy of developing new products before its competitors can. In the early 1960's Wilkenson Sword beat Gillette to the market with the stainless blade. In 1970, Wilkenson Sword introduced the bonded blade, a metal blade fused to plastic at the "optimum shaving angle."

Gillette then launched a counterattack. It introduced the first double-bladed razor, the Trac II. In 1974 it introduced Daisy, a shaver for women and in 1977, it developed Atra, the first adjustable double bladed razor.[3] In 1990, it created the Sensor and Sensor Excel. Gillette's newest product, the Mach 3, was introduced in 1998. Gillette's strategy is wait until its competition adjusts to its current product and then launches a new shaving system.

Mass—Mass the effects of overwhelming combat power at the decisive place and time.

Mass is coordinating all the elements of combat power in a short period of time where they will have maximum effect on an opposing force. Mass seeks to crush the enemy, not sting him. Massing effects, rather than concentrating forces, can enable a numerically inferior force to achieve decisive results while limiting exposure to enemy fire.

Bravo Bras, a boutique in Edina, Minnesota, receives calls nationwide from women who want a proper fitting bra. The shop's fitters will measure you, determine what size you need and choose a bra that conforms to your size and shape. "It doesn't matter what size you are," says owner Judy Anderson. "We fit the body you brought in." The company makes strapless styles for under bridal gowns and special occasion wear, maternity, nursing and sports bras. The shop is also certified by the manufacturers to fit and provide mastectomy bras.[4]

Economy of Force—Employ all combat power available in the most effective way possible; allocate minimum essential combat power to secondary efforts.

Economy of force is the judicious use and distribution of forces. No element of the force should ever be left without an assignment. When the time for action arrives, all parts must execute. The allocation of available combat power to such operations as limited attacks, defense, delays, deception, or even retrograde operations is gauged in order to achieve mass elsewhere at the decisive point and time on the battlefield.

Hewlett Packard (HP) maintains a strategy of producing new and improved products rather than extending the product life cycle and maximizing unit volume of older products. Products must make a technical contribution, they cannot be copycat products. If a product does not make a technical contribution, Hewlett Packard will not pursue it, no matter what the market potential. Consider this conversation between a veteran lab manager and an inexperienced product manager at HP in 1984:

PRODUCT MANAGER: "We've got to introduce an IBM-compatible personal computer *now.*

That's where the market is going. That's where the volume is. That's what customers primarily want."

LAB MANAGER: "But where's the technological contribution? Until we figure out a way to make an IBM-compatible personal computer with a clear technical advantage, then we just can't do it—no matter how big the market."

PRODUCT MANAGER: "But what if that's not what customers want? What if they just want to run their software and really don't care about technical contribution? And what if the market window will close unless we act now?

LAB MANAGER: "Then we shouldn't be in that business. That's not who we are. We simply shouldn't be in markets that don't value technical contribution. That's not what the Hewlett-Packard Company is all about."

When HP allocates research and development funds, the most innovative divisions get the most resources. Furthermore, manufacturing plants can only attain full divisional status by creating an innovative new product and taking it to market.[5]

Maneuver—Place the enemy in a position of disadvantage through the flexible application of combat power.

Maneuver is the movement of forces in relation to the enemy to gain positional advantage. Effective maneuver keeps the opposition off balance and protects the force. Used to exploit successes, preserve freedom of action, and reduce vulnerability, it continually creates new problems for the opposition rendering his responses ineffective, eventually leading to defeat.

At all levels of war, successful application of maneuver demands thought, plans, operations, and organizations. It requires designating and then changing points of main effort and the considered application of the principles of mass and economy of force. At the operational level maneuver is the method by which the commander determines where and when to fight by setting the terms of battle, refusing battle, or acting to take advantage of tactical actions. Maneuver is dynamic warfare that forsakes predictable patterns of operations.

When James C. Collins and Jerry I. Porras, authors of *Built to Last*, interviewed Bill Hewlett of Hewlett—Packard, they asked him if there was any company he viewed as role model. His response was: "3M! No doubt about it. You never know what they're going to come up with next. The beauty of it is that *they* probably don't know what they're going to come up with next, either. But even though you can never predict what exactly the company will do, you know that it will continue to be successful."[6]

From 1907 to 1914, 3M was struggling to survive. Its chief competitor, Norton, was ten times the size of 3M and the industry leader in bonded abrasives. However, Norton had an explicit policy of *not* pursuing new opportunities outside it traditional product lines. As one Norton research scientist recounted: Although we would play with the idea of doing research on new, radically, different products, almost all work…involved…making better grinding wheels…You could work on anything you wanted as long as it was round and had a hole in it.[7]

By 1962, 3M generated over three times the revenues and nearly twice the profit margins of Norton. While Norton had focused on old—line abrasives, 3M exploited opportunities that led to an array of products including waterproof sandpaper, masking tape, cellophane tape. 3M continued to expand with businesses such as Scotchguard fabric protector, magnetic recording tapes, microfilm and fax products. Norton still derived over 75 percent of its sales from traditional abrasives. In 1990, 3M had $13 billion in sales. Norton was acquired in a hostile takeover and ceased to exist as an independent corporation.[8]

Unity of Command—For every objective, seek unity of command and unity of effort.

At all echelons of warfare massing combat toward a command objective requires unity of command and unity of effort. Unity of command means that all the forces are under one responsible commander. It requires a single commander with the necessary authority to direct all forces in pursuit in a unified purpose.

Unity of effort requires coordination and cooperation among all forces toward a commonly recognized objective even though they may not necessarily be part of the same command structure. Main force and parallel operations might occur simultaneously united by intent and purpose, if not command. The ability to achieve unity of purpose is a nested concept where each subsequent echelon is nested in the other.

Unity of effort—coordination through cooperation and common interests—is an essential complement to unity of command.

At General Electric (GE), CEO Jack Welch sets precise performance objectives and monitors them throughout the year. Each of Welch's three vice—chairmen and twelve business chiefs receives a handwritten, two—page evaluation of his performance each year. Each business director then models the actions of his boss, and their associates do the same. For example, Lloyd G. Trotter, CEO of GE's electrical distribution and control operation held a 2½ day leadership conference with his top 250 people. When Welch reiterated the goals, Trotter then conveyed his goals to the 97 people in his organization. Other GE businesses follow a similar format. "Welch preaches from the top, and people see it at the bottom," says Thomas E. Dunham, who directs services in GE Medical Systems.[9]

Security—Never allow the enemy to acquire an unexpected advantage.

Security enhances freedom of action by reducing vulnerability to hostile acts, influence, or surprise. The actions taken by a commander to protect his forces result in security. Knowledge and understanding of enemy strategy, tactics, doctrine, and staff planning achieve the detail planning of adequate security measures. While risk is inherent in war, commanders must not be too cautious. To succeed, commanders must take calculated risks to maintain the force and defeat the enemy. Protecting the force increases friendly combat power.

In the late 1980's FedEx had successfully test marketed the concept of the overnight letter. Airborne Express also began test-marketing in similar markets in Philadelphia, Hartford, and Cleveland. FedEx entered those test markets with its own product distorting Airborne's tests and diverting customers with FedEx's better known name.[10]

Surprise—Strike the enemy at a time or place or in a manner for which is he is unprepared.

Surprise can decisively alter the balance of combat power. Utilizing surprise, forces can attain success well out of proportion to the effort expended. The opposition need not be taken completely by surprise, but only to become aware too late to react effectively. Factors contributing to surprise are: speed, sufficient intelligence, deception, application of unexpected combat power, operations security (OPSEC), and variations in tactics and methods of operation.

Surprise can also be in tempo, size of force, direction or location of main effort, and timing. In 1980, American Broadcasting Company (ABC) developed a series of extremely successful daytime dramas targeted at women. It also incorporated a sales force to specifically sell daytime television to advertisers. Combining high viewer ratings, lower advertising rates, and reduced production costs from using lower paid actors and actresses and shooting on inexpensive sets ABC both a dominant position and a high return. ABC's six daytime dramas earned an estimated 25% of ABC's sales revenues and 40% of its profits ($235 million) in 1983.[10]

Simplicity—Prepare clear, uncomplicated plans and concise orders to ensure thorough understanding.

Carl von Clausewitz said, "Everything in war is very simple, but the simplest thing is difficult." Those familiar with military operations know they are difficult to accomplish. Simple plans and clear, concise orders minimize misunderstanding and confusion. When other factors are equal, the simplest plan is preferable. Simplicity is invaluable when soldiers and leaders are tired. Simplicity in plans allow better understanding and troop leading at all echelons and permits branches and sequels to be more easily understood and executed.

Nordstrom's employee handbook consists of one five by eight-inch card:

Welcome to Nordstrom. We're glad to have you with our Company. Our number one goal is to provide **outstanding customer service.** Set both your personal and professional goals high. We have great confidence in your ability to achieve them.

Nordstrom Rules:

Rule #1: **Use your good judgement in all situations.** There will be no additional rules.

Please feel free to ask your department manager, store manager, or division general manager any question at any time.

"We view our people as sales professionals," Jim Nordstrom once told a Stanford Business School class. "They need basic guideposts, but not rules. You can do anything you need to at Nordstrom to get the job done, just so long as you live up to our basic values and standards."[11]

In 1993, General Electric's CEO Jack Welch heard some complaints about the poor quality tubes in GE's X-ray and CAT-scan machines. GE's tubes was averaging a little more than 25,000 scans, less than half what competing tubes were achieving.

To correct the problem, Welch contacted Marc Onetto, general manager for service and maintenance in Europe. Onetto's orders were simple and direct. "Fix it," Welch told Onetto. "I want 100,000 scans out of my tubes!"

During the next four years Onetto faxed weekly briefs to Welch, outlining his progress. Onetto's team has developed tubes that average between 150,000 and 200,000 scans adding about $14 million in productivity benefits to the division.[12]

When Grant Tinker took over the television network NBC in the early 1980's, it was being pounded by CBS and ABC. The network was in last place in the ratings, losing money and didn't have one hit program. Fred Silverman, Tinker's predecessor, was known as a micromanager who created chaotic working conditions. Silverman dictated the contents of the shows, chose the actors, writers and directors and made all the scheduling decisions. The result: last place in the Neilson ratings.

In contrast, Tinker, who had successfully run the Mary Tyler Moore (MTM) production company had a simple management style: Hire the best people and let them do their jobs. The result was popular shows such as *The Mary Tyler Moore Show, Lou Grant, WKRP in Cincinnati,* and *Hill Street Blues.*

Tinker revealed his strategy at the annual meeting of the NBC local station managers. "I'm going to get the best people," Tinker said, "and let them do good work." That was his strategy.

Soon after the season began, one of Tinker's first major decisions was leave an woefully rated show on the air, because he thought its producer was "good at his job." That show was *Cheers.* He also spared an even lower ranked show because he thought it producer "was good at his job." That was *Family Ties.* He allowed a hospital show that was floundering to survive because he said, he "liked it." That show was St. Elsewhere. Finally, Tinker hired an accomplished actor-producer and let him the kind of show he wanted. The person was Bill Cosby and the result was *The Cosby Show,* the most successful TV program of the 1980s. Within two years, NBC was the top rated network and still remains one of the strongest entertainment companies in the world.[13]

Summary

The nine principles of war are:

Objective—Direct every military operation toward a clearly defined, decisive, and attainable goal.

Offensive—Seize, retain, and exploit the initiative.

Mass—Mass the effects of overwhelming combat power at the decisive place and time.

Economy of force—Employ all combat power available in the most effective way possible; allocate minimum essential combat power to secondary efforts.

Maneuver—Place the enemy in a position of disadvantage through the flexible application of combat power.

Unity of command—For every objective, seek unity of command and unity of effort.

Security—Never permit the enemy to acquire unexpected advantage.

Surprise—Strike the enemy at a time or place or in a manner for which he is unprepared.

Simplicity—Prepare clear, uncomplicated plans and concise orders to ensure thorough understanding.

3. Principles of Maneuver Warfare

Before we look at how maneuver warfare can win battles, let's look at how direct frontal assaults can lose battles and waste resources. During the Korean War, Lieutenant General James A. Van Fleet ordered the capture of two mountains—Hill 983 known also as Bloody Ridge and another known as Heartbreak Ridge. Twelve artillery battalions destroyed the vegetation on the mountains. While the artillery barrage obliterated all the vegetation it did little to destroy the well-fortified bunkers of North Korean and Chinese soldiers.

The only avenues of approach on these mountains were steep and well covered by Communist fields of fire. American, South Korean, and French soldiers began climbing these steep ridges and were decimated by enemy mortars and automatic weapons fire. The United Nations Forces finally seized the summit of those peaks-but the cost was enormous. The UN forces suffered 6,400 casualties while the Communist losses were estimated at 40,000. Despite all the resources allotted to these attacks, the UN command had gained nothing. There were no tactical gains and the UN forces strategic position had not changed. The tactics used during the Korean War were identical to those used during World War I and the results were the were the same as they had been in the trenches of Europe: extensive human losses and no tangible tactical or strategic gains.[1]

Business journals are full of case studies outlining disastrous campaigns conducted by companies. Corporations often launch the military equivalent of a frontal assault with predicable results. The campaign fails miserably or the corporation expends so much of its resources it gains nothing.

Maneuver warfare relies on speed of movement, deception, surprise, and the human dimension of conflict. It does not ignore force ratios and loss rates but rather emphasizes defeating the opponent through other means than attacking his strength. It has been used successfully throughout history. Ghenghis Khan used it in his campaigns in central Asia and Eastern Europe. Napoleon Bonaparte's *manoeuvre sur les derrières* enabled him to conquer much of Europe.

Maneuver warfare, however, requires boldness and daring. During the Civil War, General Thomas J. "Stonewall" Jackson proposed a strategy to go around the Union Army and strike behind Washington at Union railways and cities, damaging the North's property so heavily that the people would grant the South its independence. However, the Confederate president Jefferson Davis rejected this daring proposal. Despite Davis' objection to the plan, Jackson eventually used a variation of this proposal during his successful campaign in the Shenadoah Valley of Virginia in the spring of 1862.[2]

In 1940, Generals Heinz Guderian and Erich Von Manstein had problems convincing the German high command to conduct it main attack through the Ardennes Forest and cross the Meuse River at Sedan before the French could establish a defense. This would place the German army behind the Allied defensive lines and allow panzers to attack immediately west towards the lower Somme and cut off all the enemy forces that had been moved into Belgium. Manstein, however, appealed to the Chancellor Adolf Hitler who approved the plan in February 1940. The campaign was extremely successful. With fewer troops and tanks, Germany defeated France and the British army in six weeks and forcing Britain to abandon much of its equipment during its evacuation at Dunkirk.[3]

Finally, General Douglas McCarthur had problems convincing Generals J. Lawton Collins, army chief of staff and Hoyt S. Vandenberg, air force chief of staff to conduct an amphibious assault at Inchon during the Korean War. Chief of staff Omar Bradley agreed with Collins and Vadenberg. Bradley would later write "I had to agree that it was the riskiest military proposal I had ever heard of. Inchon was probably the worst place ever selected for an amphibious landing."[4]

The three methods of maneuver warfare are:

1. Preemption: Neutralizing the enemy before the conflict has begun.
2. Dislocation: Demphasizing the enemy's strength.
3. Disruption: defeating the enemy by successfully attacking his center of gravity.[5]

PREEMPTION

The term preemption is derived from the Latin word *praeemere*, meaning "to buy beforehand." It also means "to seize or appropriate for oneself before others."

Preemptive strikes are often viewed negatively. The reason is that preemption is a move that occurs before its time. A commander employing preemption relies on rapid decision-making, speed and surprise rather than caution, careful deliberation, and methodical movement. He may be numerically stronger or weaker than his opponent; his weapons may be superior or inferior; his doctrine may be ingenious or flawed; but the one asset he possesses is resolve. He attempts to snatch a victory before the battle has begun.[6]

One example of preemption is the 1967 war between Israel and Egypt. Often called the Six-Day War, the outcome of the war was decided in one day. Events leading up to the 1967 war were an alliance between Egypt, Iraq, Syria, and Jordan. Gamal Nasser, president of Egypt did two things to provoke action by Israel. He closed the Strait of Tiran to Israeli shipping and he formed an offensive military alliance with states bordering Israel.

The Israeli command decided to conduct a preemptive strike. On June 5, 1967, almost the entire Israeli Air Force launched an attack against Egyptian airfields in the Sinai, along the Suez Canal, the Red Sea, and certain sites in Nile Delta and Nile Valley. Most of the Egyptian Air Force officers seemed to be caught between home and base during these attacks. The pilots who managed to reach their planes were killed or wounded when they were struck. The Egyptian planes that did manage to get in the air were soon shot down. The Egyptians lost approximately 300 of their 500 first-line aircraft. Having established air superiority, the Israeli army launched a series of ground attacks. The speed of the ground attacks threw the opposition completely off balance that what started as an Egyptian retreat turned into a rout.[7]

In the business world, fast cycle times are one way to preempt your competition. The Japanese have been utilizing fast cycle times to get their new products to market before their rivals since the 1980's.

For example, every year between 1979 and 1988, the Mitsubishi Electric Company added a new feature or made a major design change to its 3-horsepower pump. In 1980, Mitsubishi introduced integrated circuits to control the heat pump cycle-fifteen years before an American company even considered the concept of integrated circuits for their residential heat pumps.

Even if the U.S firm had pursued the concept, it would have taken four to five years to bring the product to market and the American company would only have developed in 1990 a heat pump comparable to the 1980 Melco heat pump. The result was the American company gave up on the idea and purchased its advanced air conditioners, heat pumps and components from the Japanese competition.[8]

In volatile markets, such as women's fashion, fast-cycle business strategies reduce risk. Clothing orders from the Far East can require lead times of up to nine months with demand being as much as 40% above or below long-range forecasts. Some U.S. clothing manufacturers have shortened their lead times to weeks reducing forecasting inaccuracies to 10%. Milkliken & Co., a textile manufacturer can deliver fabric to a customer in a week or less. Nicolle Miller, a men's and women's apparel manufacturer, began moving operations back to the U.S. in 1986. Now most of its suits and dresses are made in the United States.[9]

Breweries also used preemption when they introduced ice beers into the American market. Although Budeweiser's share of the U.S. beer market is 44.1%, it was slow to develop an ice beer. However, Miller Brewing Company with its emphasis on fast cycle time and very local marketing attention, introduced Icehouse and Icehouse Lite. By getting Icehouse and Icehouse Lite widely distributed before Anheuser-Busch could launch a comparable brand, Miller captured over 50% of the ice beer sales in supermarkets while Anheuser-Busch's share was 29%.

Miller accomplished this with a concept called <u>momentum market-ing</u>. With momentum marketing you conduct six simple tests rather than launching one or two large-scale product trials each year requiring expensive TV commercials and retail displays. Miller ships the prototype brew and promotional items to approximately 15 bars and restaurants in a few select cities. Its marketers observe customers, interview bartenders, and then conduct telephone surveys of patrons who fill out cards at the bar. This allowed Miller to test Icehouse beer inexpensively-$500,000 vs. $12 million to try out a comparable new product in 1993.[10]

DISLOCATION

Dislocation is the art of neutralizing the enemy's strength. Rather than fighting the hostile force on its terms, the friendly force avoids any combat in which the enemy can effectively utilize its strength.[11]

The Hussite Revolution in 1420 pitted King Sigismund and his aristocratical supporters against an alliance of disaffected nobles and peasant armies of religious dissent. The challenges facing Count Jan Zizka were formidable. First, he only had a few hundred farmers equipped with flails (used to thrash wheat) to fight Sigismund's well-equipped knights. Furthermore, his men were untrained and unlikely to maintain their cohesion when defending against a charge by mounted knights.

Zizka noted that knights had a weakness. When field fortifications forced the knights to dismount, the knight's main strength—mounted shock action—was neutralized. In addition, the heavily armored knights were clumsy on foot and tired easily. However, Zizka was not conducting a defensive operation. To free Bohemia from its oppressors required an offensive operation and conventional field fortifications could not be picked up and moved.

However, the Hussite peasants had wagons and carts as part of their logistical train. Zizka would lead his army into enemy territory spreading mayhem throughout the towns. The enemy would then send an army to chase the Hussites. Zizka would then find a defensible piece of terrain, usually a hilltop, and circle his wagons. He then chained them together and anchored large shields in the gaps between the wagons. The wagons had been modified to provide firing ports for the small arms and crossbows his army had gradually acquired. When the enemy charged, their formations broke up. If the knights dismounted and tried to breach the wagons, the Hussites would stab the isolated knights through the portals with spears. When the enemy finally withdrew,

Zizka would unchain his wagons and pursue the fleeing knights with his small cavalry reserve.[12]

Budwieser, controlled 44% of U.S. beer sales in 1994. It has introduced relatively few new products. In 1994, August Busch IV, vice president of brand management said: "The breweries we have are designed to produce big brands. Our system is set up to sell big brands. Our competition can't compete with big brands. That's why they've had to introduce lots of little brands."

Which is exactly what Miller Brewing did. Miller, who controlled 22% of the U.S. market in 1994, broadened its portfolio of brands by purchasing Molsen Breweries USA It also raised its output of new beers from an average of two per year to seven in 1994.

Miller also changed to a more flexible brewing system. It studied how Bass Brewers, Britain's leading brewer had refashioned its brewery to handle multiple, low volume products. Miller concluded that it did not need a new brewery with small kettles and flexible production lines. Instead the company spent $500 million to retool its six big plants. Shifting production from one beer to another used to take four hours. It now takes one.[13]

Currently, concrete is the material of choice when building a basement. However, concrete basements have two drawbacks: cold in the winter and damp in the summer. Wayne Kimber Jr., a former block layer and ready-mix concrete seller, started Woodmaster Foundations. Woodmaster designs, fabricates, hauls and installs treated wood foundations at building sites in several states.

While wood foundations cost about 5 percent more than concrete, it offers better insulating properties from the cold and is easier to finish. The walls are made from yellow pine planks and plywood treated with chromated copper arsenate (CCA). CCA is a pressure-treated wood approved by the Environmental Protection Agency for use in residential structures. It is also used for decks and picnic tables.

Engineered for strength and durability the walls stand 8 feet 4.5 inches tall and are made of 3/4 inch plywood fastened with nonrusting nails to 2-by-6 studs. Horizontal seams are ship-lapped and glued for tightness. The firm gives a 15-year limited warranty against leaks and a 75-year limited warranty against deterioration caused by termites or fungal decay. According to Kimber, "In wet 1993, we had one call-back on a leak with 2,000 basements out there in nine states."[14]

DISRUPTION

Disruption is the technique of subduing the enemy by attacking his critical vulnerability. Destroying or neutralizing that vulnerability paralyzes the opponent's forces. The goal of disruption is to defeat the opposition by rendering his forces ineffective by locating and striking his weakness. This avoids having to destroy the adversary's entire force by direct attack.[15]

Contrary to popular belief, the Germans did not have superior numbers when they invaded France in 1940. Although they had fewer and less powerful tanks than their opponents, their armor offensives proved decisive. Only in airpower, the most important factor, did they have superiority.

The German invasion of the West began with attacks into the Netherlands and Belgium. Rotterdam, its communications center and The Hague, its capital, were attacked early May 10 by airborne forces. Their main mission was to capture bridges at Rotterdam, Dordrecht, and Moerdijk, before the Dutch could blow them up and keep them open until the arrival of ground forces. The objective of the secondary attack on The Hague was to capture the leaders of the Government and Services in their offices and disrupt administrative functions. Although this attack was repelled, it caused much confusion.

Luftwaffe bombings added to the widespread panic and disorder these twin assaults to the front and rear of Holland created. Exploiting the chaos, German armored elements maneuvered through a break in the southern flank and rendezvoused with airborne units at Rotterdam three days later. On the fifth day the Dutch surrendered, although their main line was still intact.[16]

In Belgium, General von Reichenau's 6th Army had the formidable mission of capturing two bridges over the Albert Canal and Fort Eben Emael, Belgium's most modern base. The fort at Eben Emael was designed to confront every threat except the possibility of enemy troops landing on top of it. General Student had only 500 airborne troops left to assist with this mission.

A detachment of 78 airborne engineers commanded by Lieutenant Witzig executed the surprise attack on Fort Eben Emael. This small group of paratroopers landed on the roof, overpowered the anti-aircraft crew, and destroyed the armored cupolas and casemates of the weapons with a new potent explosive transported by a freight carrying glider. From the roof, the soldiers held off the garrison of 1,200 men until German ground forces arrived twenty-four hours later.

The Belgian guards on the two key bridges were taken by surprise. At one bridge, they actually lit the fuse to blow it up-but the crew of a glider fought its way into the blockhouse and extinguished the fuse before it could detonate. It should also be noted that on the whole invasion front the bridges were destroyed, according to plan, except where the airborne troops were employed.[16]

Meanwhile, Rundstedt's Army Group maneuvered through a seventy-mile stretch of the Ardennes in Luxembourg and Belgian Luxembourg towards France. Many conventional strategists had long regarded this area as "impassable" for an armor operation. However, this increased the probability of surprise since the dense forests helped obscure the advance and disguise the strength of the operation. On the fourth day of the offensive, they arrived on the banks of the Meuse.

⌈The French attempted to counterattack. However, the French High Command, trained in the slower tactics of World War I, could not contend with the speed of the panzers' pace, paralyzing the French commanders⌋ Immobilized by the speed of the German advances, 120,000 French soldiers died and 1.5 million soldiers were taken prisoner. Many French units were combat effective when they surrendered. They had suffered relatively few casualties, most of their equipment was intact, and they had sufficient supplies to continue fighting. French doctrine, however, had not prepared its commanders for the tempo of modern warfare.[18]

In 1968, 7-UP's strategy was to position its lemon-line beverage as the Uncola, an alternative to Coke and Pepsi. The first year sales rose 15 percent. Ten years later, Philip Morris bought 7-UP for $520 million.

7-UP needed to find a weakness in Coke's and Pepsi's defense. It found it the colas' strength, the cola nut. In order to call a beverage a cola it must contain caffeine. It's a Food and Drug Administration regulation.

Jack Trout and Al Ries presented a "no caffeine" campaign to Seven-Up in 1980. The prototype television commercial said "You wouldn't give your kid a cup of coffee. Then why give the kid a can of cola which contains just as much caffeine? Give her the Uncola, Uncaffeine soft drink 7-UP."

At first, Seven-up's marketing department resisted the idea. "Never will we promote our product that way," said a marketing vice-president. However, in early 1982 Seven-Up instituted the "no caffeine" campaign "Never had it, never will."

The "no caffeine" strategy did what a disruption campaign should do; it created confusion and turmoil in the ranks of Coke and Pepsi. "Seven-Up ads on caffeine rile industry," wrote the *Wall Street Journal*. In an official statement, PepsiCo called Seven-UP's ad campaign "a disservice to the public, since it perpetuates unsubstantiated health concerns by use of scare tactics." In addition, the Pepsi maker stated it is "firmly convinced" that caffeine poses no health risk.

However, six months later PepsiCo introduced regular and diet versions of cola called Pepsi Free. Others soon followed. Coca-Cola, Royal Crown, Dr. Pepper, and SunKist took out the caffeine. Other brands that never had caffeine such as Sprite and Canada Dry ginger ale started to say so.[19]

Another example of disruption is the Cable News Network (CNN). Most media deliver the news at their convenience. For example, the newspapers arrive around 5 a.m. each day. Unless a very special event occurs such as the first few days of the Gulf War or the O.J. Simpson verdict, the TV networks give you the news at 6:30 or 7:00 p.m. (EST) whether you want it or not. If you live west of Chicago you receive the regurgitated news one to three hour later.

CNN's philosophy is "delivering news on demand." It views the news as an "ever revolving news wheel." A new story is added. An old story may disappear. The preceding hour's lead story might be updated. The "news wheel" keeps evolving.

CNN produces its news in a different manner than the traditional networks. A reporter with a traditional network is a specialist, covers a maximum of one story, and is supported with a large crew of directors, lighting, and camera personnel. They focus on a small number of stories. Story assignments are often received from an executive producer in New York. At CNN, often a video journalist (VJ) will report on two or three stories a day and often covers a story with just a cameraperson, possibly a soundperson. The VJ is a multi-skilled person who does most of the writing, directs the broadcast, and may do the sound. The assignment desk or one of the bureaus will surface a story. After an informal tentative signoff from Earl Casey, executive vice-president for news gathering or Earl Casey, vice-president and managing editor domestic, the assignment desk calls the lead bureau and speaks directly with the video journalist who will be doing the story asking the most important question; "can you get it done in 24 hours?"

CNN went on the air June 1, 1980. That day it tallied its first scoop. It covered President Jimmy Carter—live—emerging from Vernon Jordan's hospital room after an assassination attempt on the civil rights leader. (Incidentally, CNN had paid for a satellite link to Fort Wayne until 6:30 p.m. Mr. Carter departed the hospital at 6:22 p.m. Had he left Vernon Jordan's room eight minutes later, CNN would have lost its satellite link and the story.)

Other breaking news CNN covered in its early days were the assassination attempts on President Ronald Reagan and Pope John Paul II, the fire at the MGM Grand Hotel in Las Vegas, and the collapse of the walkway at the Kansas City Hyatt Hotel.[20]

THE ENVELOPMENT

The envelopment, sometimes known as the flanking attack, is a basic technique used in maneuver warfare that applies strength against weakness. It is the preferred form of maneuver. In an envelopment, the attacker avoids the enemy's front where forces are most protected and fields of fires are most easily concentrated. To perform an envelopment, an assailable flank must be found. This requires detail and aggressive reconnaissance.[21] Napoleon Bonaparte's *manoeuve sur les derrièeres* employed during the Marengo campaign in Italy of 1800 and the opening stages of the Austerlitz campaign of 1805 are variations of the flanking maneuver. General Douglas McCarthur's landing at Inchon is another example of the flanking maneuver.

The envelopment is a devastating maneuver for several reasons. First, if the opponent is compelled to change his front, he tends to be dislocated and unable to fight effectively.

When the envelopment is properly executed in business, the results can be spectacular. However, the envelopment is a difficult concept to sell to businesses because there is no established market for the new product or service. In order for an envelopment to be successful in business, three things must occur:
1. It must be made into an uncontested territory.
2. It must contain the element of surprise.
3. Once success is achieved, it must be sustained.

One of the classic business flanking maneuvers is Miller's introduction of Miller Lite in 1975. While a few regional "light" beers existed, there were no national light beers. Most of the light brands launched failed.

Lite completely surprised its competition. There were no rumors in the press nor was there any test marketing. It was launched as quickly as possible. It took a year for Schlitz to respond with Schlitz Light and 2 years for Anheuser-Busch to introduce Natural Light.

Finally, its success was sustained. Miller flooded the media with commercials, spending four times the industry's per-barrel average. Three years after the introduction of Lite, there were 22 other light brands on the market.[22]

Lite rose to America's Number 2 beer with sales at 19.9 million and 10.3% share. However, by 1996 shipments had dropped to 15.9 million barrels and a market share of 8.5%. One possible reason is the Anheuser-Busch supported its brand, Bud Light, while Miller exhausted it resources pursuing temporary niches.[23] → *success not sustained*

Another example of the envelopment is Boeing's development of the 707. In 1952, Boeing's engineers had the idea to build a large jet aircraft for the commercial market. However, no aircraft company had proven there was a market for jet aircraft. Boeing's rival, Douglas Aircraft projected that propeller-driven aircraft would continue to dominate the market. At that time, Boeing's primary customer was the U.S. Air Force

and its earlier attempts to enter the commercial market had been failures. As a result, it had virtually no presence in the commercial aircraft
market. To develop a jet aircraft prototype would cost the company three
times Boeing's annual after-tax profit for the past five years-approxi-
mately one fourth of its entire corporate net worth. Furthermore, commercial airlines expressed little interest in purchasing a jet from Boeing.
(Boeing builds great bombers, period). [24]

Boeing decided to build the jet and named it the 707. The jet brought
the commercial aircraft business into the jet age and established the
company as major player in the commercial aircraft industry. In contrast, Douglas Aircraft (later to become McDonnell-Douglas) made a
definitive decision to adhere with manufacturing piston propeller aircraft. Douglas waited and watched Boeing capture control of the commercial market. As airlines rushed to replace their piston planes in
1957, Douglas Aircraft still did not have a jet ready for the market.
Finally, in 1958, Douglas introduced the DC-8, but was never able to
catch Boeing.

Boeing could have become complacent and rested on the success of
the 707. However, Sun Tzu warns "Now to win battles and take your
objectives, but to fail to exploit these achievements is ominous and may
be described as 'wasteful delay.'"

Boeing heeded this advice and continued to innovate. In the early
1960's Eastern Airlines approached Boeing to design a new jet. Build a
jet that could land on runway 4-22 at La Guardia Airport (only 4,860
feet long-much too short for any existing passenger jet) and be able to
fly nonstop from New York to Miami. In addition, it had to be wide
enough for six-abreast seating, have a capacity of 131 passenger and
meet Boeing's high standards of durability. The result was the 727, a sig-
nificant breakthrough in aircraft technology. Boeing's original market
estimate for the 727 was 300 planes. Eventually, the company sold over
1800 and the 727 became the short range choice of the airline industry.

Finally, in 1965, Boeing made one of the most daring business moves in aviation history: the decision to build the 747 jumbo jet. Boeing Chairman William Allen declared "we will build this airplane, we will build it even if takes the resources of the entire company!" The project nearly killed the company when in the early 1970's sales of the 747 grew more slowly the expected. During the period from 1969 to 1971, Boeing laid off a total of eighty-six thousand people, approximately 60 percent of the company's workforce.[25]

Summary

Maneuver warfare attempts to defeat the enemy through means other than attacking his strength.

The three types of maneuver warfare are preemption, dislocation, and disruption.

Preemption relies on rapid decision-making, speed and surprise rather than caution, careful deliberation, and methodical movement.

Dislocation is the ability to render the opponent's strength irrelevant.

Disruption is the technique of subduing the enemy by destroying or neutralizing his critical vulnerability and paralyzing the opponent's forces.

The envelopment is a basic technique used in maneuver warfare. The attacker strikes the opposition's flank or rear causing the enemy to fight from a direction from which he is less prepared.

4. Guerrilla Operations

Guerrilla warfare is a weapon a nation inferior in arms and military equipment can use against more powerful well-equipped adversary. Guerrilla operations allow a force to conceal its primary weakness, the lack of sustained hitting power and utilize its strength: the ability to quickly appear at the time and place of its choosing, surprising the enemy.[1]

Guerrilla warfare is a defensive tactic. The critical difference between conventional warfare and guerrilla warfare is guerrillas don't maintain a battle line. Operating in the enemy's rear area, guerrillas must rely upon an amiable population to feed, sustain, and sometimes hide them. This means that guerrilla warfare can only succeed in one's own country. An aggressor invading another country cannot conduct a guerrilla war because the local people are certain to be hostile.

Although the invaded country's forces may be inadequate to those of the invading army's it does not have to surrender. It can move to guerrilla war and prevent the invader from achieving victory. It may take time and will be costly, but the guerrilla can produce a stalemate. In time, the invader will withdraw rather than face the slow draining of resources and heavy expenditures that a stalemate creates.[2]

There have been many successful guerrilla leaders throughout history. One of the most adept of them was Francis Marion, "the Swamp Fox." Marion was a farmer who grew up in South Carolina and had little formal education. In 1759, he joined a regiment raised to fight the Cherokees, who were raiding the borders of the Carolinas. During the course of these hostilities he accumulated his mind many of the tactics he would later use against the British.

When the Revolutionary War broke out, Marion immediately accepted a commission in the Second South Carolina Regiment. By 1780 he had seen enough of the war to recognize that the Continental Army was overlooking a very advantageous field—guerilla warfare. Marion obtained permission to raise a company that at first was composed of twenty ill-equipment men and boys.

Marion's guerrilla operations in North and South Carolina took a heavy toll on the British commander, Major General Earl Cornwallis, whose attempts to pacify those two states were constantly hampered. Operating from bases in the nearly inaccessible swamps, Marion attacked isolated garrisons, convoys, and trains. His information was always timely and correct since he had the support of the people. Unable to contend with Marion's tactics, the British labeled him a criminal, and complained bitterly that he neither fought like "gentleman nor like a Christian."[3]

Vo Nyguyen Giap, general of the Vietminh (national independence movement) successfully used guerrilla warfare against the French in the 1950s. Incorporating the principles of the Chinese strategist Sun Tzu, Giap avoided the enemy when he was strong and attacked him when he was weak. Concentrating his troops at an exposed enemy point, Giap could achieve superior firepower in a "in a given place, and at a given time." He then exercised the same techniques against the United States when it entered the conflict in 1965, successfully adapting to American firepower and mobility, including the helicopter-borne soldiers who could land and dismount at almost any point they chose.

Like Mao Tse-Tung, Giap realized that a guerrilla war alone would never insure defeat of the opposition. He viewed guerrilla warfare as a stage to diminish the stamina and resolution of the French. Once the French were sufficiently weakened and demoralized, the Vietminh would then employ conventional warfare tactics and defeat the French.[4]

In the business world, most companies should be waging guerrilla warfare. Out of 100 companies, as a general rule, one should play defense, two should play offensive, three should flank, and 94 should be guerrillas.[5]

A guerrilla business finds a avoids direct competition with big businesses. For example, James Belasco, co-author of the book *Flight of the Buffalo*, owned a textile coloring company that was competing with a foreign company who was paying five cents an hour in wages and was being subsidized by its government. Yet Belasco's textile coloring business continued to prosper. It chose a niche where low-cost labor didn't count, focusing its efforts on solving manufacturer's and dyer's tough coloring problems.

Guerrillas come in all shapes and sizes. In many metropolitan areas, besides the large daily newspapers, there are often small weekly newspapers. These newspapers report news in the local community that the larger daily papers cannot cover. In the classified section of these newspapers, many small businesses serving the local area advertise here. These plumbers, painters, carpenters, tree surgeons, snowplow operators, and excavators often operate in a small geographic area.

Weather Watch, Inc. is a company in Minnesota that predicts local weather at three-hour intervals and notifies subscribers about impending severe weather before it arrives. Founded by Amy Rolando, a former TV meteorologist, Weather Watch has 19 local communities and 80 local businesses as clients.

Rolando got the idea for a weather service while attending the U.S. Open golf tournament at Hazeltine National Golf Club in Chaska, Minnesota when lightning killed a spectator. Rolando was astonished to learn that the tournament's weather report originated from a weather service in Pennsylvania.

During emergency weather situations, Weather Watch using state of the art technology, sends updates as often as every 15 minutes via computer or taped message.

Subscribers swear by its constant updates. "Weather Watch can save us hundreds of dollars because we know in advance what [chemical] materials to used depending on the amount of snow and when the temperatures will drop," said a director of street maintenance in Minnetonka, Minnesota.[6]

5. Staff Operations

Before your organization can preempt, dislocate, or disrupt the opposition, its departments must be able to work together as single unit. In the Army, the staff sections are divided into four general areas: Gl (Administration), G2 (Intelligence), G3 (Operations), G4 (Logistics). In the military, these areas are coordinated by the G3. A force cannot fight a battle if it does not have people, information, plans, and supplies.

Like the military, every business, from the sole proprietorship to the multinational corporation also addresses these areas. A production line cannot operate if it doesn't have the people and the raw materials to build the product. The manufactured product cannot be sold if the company does not know who its customers are. In business language, the Human Resources Department, Accounting, and Payroll are the Gl. Sales and Marketing are the G2, Operations is the G3, and Purchasing, Shipping, and Receiving are the G4. Let's further examine each of these areas.

STAFF SECTIONS

In the Army, the staff sections are divided into four general areas: Gl (Administration), G2 (Intelligence), G3 (Operations), G4 (Logistics). For example, the Human Resources Department, Accounting, and Payroll are the Gl. Sales and Marketing are the G2, Operations is the G3, and Purchasing, Shipping, and Receiving are the G4.

ADMINISTRATION

People are your most precious asset; neglect them and you're doomed to fail.
—Colonel John G. Meyer, author of Company Command, the
Bottom Line.

The Gl is the commander's principle staff officer on matters concerning human resources. The Gl responsibilities include:
—Personnel replacement. This includes monitoring unit strength and personnel replacement management. Personnel services such as strength accountability, casualty reporting, evaluation reports, promotions, orders, classification and reclassification, personnel assignment, and awards.
—Essential financial support.
—Rest, recuperation, and leave policies.[1]

There are many ways to recruit the people your business needs. For example, at Motorola every job candidate, even those looking for production line work, go through three days of interviews. During that time, applicants write a composition and take 4 1/2 hour tests in math, problem solving, and ability to work on a team. Only one candidate in ten makes the cut. Southwest Airlines uses a different approach. Southwest has found that informal interviews yield more information than rigid one-on-one meetings.[2]

James Belasco, consultant and co-author of the book *Fight of the Buffalo*, suggests organizing around your or other people's weaknesses. As people grow and develop, new strengths and weaknesses will emerge. Then reorganize.

When First Bank System Bank of Minneapolis announced it was acquiring American Bank of Mankato, David Knopick, president of tiny

Security State Bank of Mankato saw the merger as an opportunity rather than a threat.

Knopick assumed there would be both employee and customer fears and uncertainties about the consolidation. He began recruiting key American Bank employees and eventually hired five of them, including a head teller and a senior loan officer, both of whom knew nearly everyone in town. He then purchased a few newspaper ads to announce his new personnel additions just in case any of American Bank's customers wanted to follow them to Security State.

Security State's assets rose 41 percent since the end of 1993 to about $55 million. The bank's growth rate in deposits nearly doubled during the same period, to about 9 percent a year and the growth rate for loans has more than tripled to 32 percent a year. Its net earnings, which had been growing at an annual rate of 12 percent in the five preceding years, grew at a rate of 40 percent in 1994 and 1995.[3]

During periods of full employment, it can be difficult to find qualified workers. Many businesses are finding quality employees from an unexpected source: the non-traditional workforce.

Nontraditional employees are former welfare recipients, felons, and immigrants who are often considered unemployable. Nontraditional workers helped Marie Kennedy, president of Award Baking International fill additional shifts in the fall of 1993 before the beginning of the busy holiday season. The company had recently acquired new equipment and had no one to operate it. "Our backs were to the wall," said Kennedy. "We needed not one, but two shifts.

Kennedy found help from Eastside Employment Network in Minneapolis, Minnesota, an organization that helps unemployed residents find jobs. They provided her with six people, three of whom are still with the company. One recently received a promotion.

Kennedy had to breach to roadblocks when she began hiring nontraditional workers. The first barrier was language. Most of her new employees had recently immigrated from Guatemala and Mexico. She solved the problem using charts, gestures and some Spanish. "They knew a little bit of English and I knew a bit of Spanish," she said.

The second barrier was fear of the unknown. Kennedy, who was not used to working this type of labor force, wondered what kind of employees they would be. Her reservations quickly disappeared. "These people are good, steady workers," she said. "They are reliable and take pride in producing a quality product."[4]

INTELLIGENCE

Great advantage is drawn from knowledge of your adversary, and when you know the measure of his intelligence and character you can use it to play on his weakness.
　　　　　　　　　　　　　　　　—Fredrick the Great, 1747.

Intelligence has played an important part in many battles. The Battle of Midway during World War II is one example. The Japanese had superiority in force. However, Admiral Nimitz had one advantage—good intelligence. His three carriers, with 233 planes, were stationed north of Midway to be out of sight of Japanese reconnaissance planes. However, the carriers could still monitor Japanese movements from the long range Catalinas in Midway.[5]

Ignoring intelligence can be detrimental. During World War II, the British Intelligence Service warned the Russians of Hitler's impending attack of Russia. It had even predicted the exact date of the invasion. However, Stalin chose to ignore the warnings and on June 22, 1941, Hitler invaded Russia. The Red Army's initial defeats can partially be attributed to it being taken by surprise by Germany's Panzer Armies.[6]

Information is not necessarily intelligence. Intelligence is analyzed information that provides an accurate picture of the situation. Information is gathered and analyzed from a number of sources-units in contact with the enemy, patrols, cavalry units, electronic warfare units, field artillery radars, and the local population. Government agencies and the unit's higher levels of command also provide information. Soldiers are taught the SALUTE format when reporting information-Size, Activity, Location, Unit, Equipment.

In the Army, the G2 is the staff officer responsible for all military intelligence (MI) matters. The G2 acquires, analyzes, and evaluates all information and data; and presents the evaluations and recommendations to the commander.[7]

Businesses also need to utilize intelligence. David Harkleroad of the Connecticut-based Futures Group says "The smart companies are realizing they can't afford not to do competitor intelligence. Intelligence is more than just knowing the opponent. It can help locate narrow markets and prevent a company from moving into an overcrowded market or from wasting research and development money on projects competitors have abandoned.

While Sales and Marketing is primarily responsible for "intelligence" in business, it often focuses only on the market, and forgets about the competition or the company's current customers.

James A. Belasco, co-author of the book *Flight of the Buffalo*, outlined this intelligence incident. His specialty chemical company was manufacturing chemicals for a leading textile plant. A competitor then came out with a very inexpensive substitute and he lost the account.

Belasco analyzed the incident. He then realized he had ignored all of the indicators. His competitor had been building his plant for two years and there were articles in the trade journals about him entering the market. Labs had tested some of his early product and had reported the results in the technical literature. Belasco had also known that his competitor was being substantially subsidized by his government so his prices would be low.

Belasco instituted a system called scan, clip, review technique used both by John Nalsbitt, author of *Megatrends,* and the CIA. This method is also similar to the intelligence cycle used by the military. The cycle includes planning, collection, processing, and dissemination. Each person in the company scans ten magazines he or she does not normally read each month. These could range from highly technical magazines such as *Design News* to popular magazines as *Rolling Stone.*

Next, the person clips all material he or she finds interesting regarding future trends such as articles, opinion letters, or advertisements. These are placed in a file folder.

Third, the company is divided into seven review cells. Monthly, people circulate their file folders to the other members of their cell so everyone reviews the material from all seven folders.

Quarterly, the members of the review cell meet and discuss the important trends they noticed in the clipped material they reviewed. The discussion is based on three questions:

1. What is the future event that will have the greatest impact on the business?
2. What will occur when that event happens?
3. What can we do now to prepare for that event?[8]

Besides trying to predict trends, businesses must "know their enemy." Harvey Mackay, CEO and chairman of Mackay Envelope Corporation, uses the following competitive profile to help their salespersons:

1. **Pedigree**
   Name of company
   Headquarters Location
   Subsidiary or independent?
   If subsidiary, of whom?
   Publicly/privately held

2. **Physical Scale**
   Number of plants
   Plant locations

Number of employees
Geographic areas they serve best
Geographic areas they serve adequately

3. Performance as an Investment
Date fiscal year ends
LY revenues
LY profits
Performance trend the past two to three years
Unusual financial issues (heavy inventories, ect.)
D&B rating
Overall financial condition (Strong—Satisfactory—Shaky)

4. Pricing
Pricing attitude
High and mighty
Down and dirty
How do they respond to pricing competition?

5. People
Unionized (if so, by whom)
Two to three most important players in the firm and their positions
Reputation as an employer

6. Positioning
Target market
Unique products (features) offered
Firm's short-term strategy
Firm's long-term strategy

7. Plans
Do they want to hold position/grow aggressively?
Are they targeting an acquisition/rumor acquisition/merger candidate?
Product or service developments

8. Performance as a Supplier
Average delivery time
Quality of service
Service strengths
Service weaknesses
Hard/easy to resolve customer problems
What accounts do they have the best relationship?
What accounts would it hurt them the most to lose?
Entertainment, gifts, ect. practices
Their most important suppliers
Business practices reputation:
   a. Fully aboveboard
   b. Less than perfect

9. Prestige in the Business Community
Overall reputation
Has this firm (or its principals) had any legal or image problems?
Does the firm (or its parent) have any strong charitable, social, or civic involvement?
How about the top management of the company?
How is the company regarded within our industry?
How do our trade associations regard them?
10. Probing for Data
Recently recruited employees recruited from this competitor who should be debriefed

Customers who either used this competitor in the past or used them in conjunction with us who are reliable information sources about this firm

Other persons who can supply information about this company

How this company perceives us (lazy, aggressive, technically superior, etc.)

Recent articles in the trade, financial, or general press

11. Them and Us

What accounts do they have that we want?

Who is/are their salesperson(s) for these accounts?

What piece of the business (territory, market segment, ect.) do they operate in? How can we profitably grow our share?

Have we or anyone else ever won business from this company before? If yes, how was it done.

12. Post-mortem

We will beat this competitor if we do the following five things right:

A.

B.

C.

D.

E.[9]

Just as every soldier is responsible for reporting information, employees should also be responsible for providing information. For instance, competitor's salespersons love to brag about new customers. Your customers, their potential customers, may be involved in testing of a new product. Talk with them to see what the competition is planning. In addition, trade magazines, research and technical journals often reveal a competitor's plans before any product announcements.

While intelligence is primarily gathering information about your opponent, it also requires you prevent the enemy from gathering information about you. All military personnel are trained in operations security (OPSEC).

According to Senator Arlen Specter (R-Pa.), Chairman of the Senate Intelligence Committee, at least 51 nations, including Japan, China, Russia, Israel, France, and Germany have deployed spies in the U.S. to steal proprietary information from largely unsuspecting American companies.

"U.S. businesses are losing $100 billion a year because of foreign spying," said Specter. "Job losses are estimated to be over 6 million in this decade alone due to economic espionage."[10] The consequences of not protecting trade secrets can be devastating. In the early 1990's Ellery Systems, Inc. developed a sophisticated communications software for NASA. The company was about to commercialize it when the source code for the software was surreptitiously acquired by a Chinese competitor.

Unable to compete with the much larger Chinese company that was mass-producing its software faster and more cheaply in China, Ellery Systems went out of business in 1994. An FBI investigation concluded that Ellery had been the victim of a carefully orchestrated espionage operation. It also found that the Chinese company had paid a former Ellery employee $550,000 to turn over copies of the company's software and other proprietary information. However, since no federal statute directly addresses economic espionage or the protection of proprietary information, neither the former Ellery employee nor the Chinese company that stole the software will probably ever be prosecuted.[11]

Even if a company's proprietary secrets are not misappropriated, revealing its plans to its competition of its intentions can undermine a corporate strategy. For example, in the early 1970's, Johnson & Johnson McNeil Laboratories began marketing the acetaminophen product under the brand name Tylenol. It cost 50 percent more than aspirin and was sold primarily to health care specialists.

As Tylenol's sales increased, Bristol-Myers saw an opportunity. Bristol-Meyers introduced Datril with the "same pain reliever, same safety of Tylenol." The difference was the price. Datril's price was quoted at $1.85 per 100 tablets compared to Tylenol's $2.85 per 100 tablets.[12]

However, Bristol-Meyers decided to test market Datril in its traditional test markets, Albany and Peoria. However, Johnson & Johnson was watching and it immediately counterattacked. Two weeks before Datril advertising was to broadcast, Johnson & Johnson notified Bristol-Meyers it was cutting Tylenol's price to match Datril's. In addition, it also issued credit memorandums to reduce prices on existing stocks in stores.

Though Bristol-Meyers had lost the element of surprise, its primary advantage in trying to establish Datril in the market, Bristol-Meyers launched its campaign anyway. They advanced the broadcast date of the television commercials so they ran the day after they were notified of the Tylenol price reduction, assuming it would take days for the price change to be communicated down to the nation's 165,000 retail outlets.

The Datril campaign was a failure, never achieving more than one percent market share. Johnson & Johnson complained to the networks, the magazines, the Proprietary Association, and the Council of Better Business Bureaus.

The networks asked for changes in the advertisements. First, the "dollar lower" price was changed to "Datril can cost less, a lot less." Later, "a lot less" was deleted. Finally, CBS and NBC refused to run Datril ads at all.[11]

Bristol-Meyers made two tactical errors. First, it ignored Sun Tzu's axiom "Probe him and learn where his strength is abundant and where deficient." It should have learned where Tylenol was strong in the market.

It should have then quietly launched Datril in market areas where Tylenol was not established or was weak.

It also ignored Sun Tzu's axiom "The enemy must not know where I intend to give battle. For if he does not know where I intend to give battle he must prepare in a great many places. And when he prepares in a great many places, those I have to fight in any one place will be few."

When Bristol-Meyers test-marketed Datril it alerted Johnson & Johnson of its intentions and allowed Johnson & Johnson to take defensive measures. The element of surprise was Bristol-Meyers only advantage and that was lost when it test-marketed Datril. Had Bristol-Meyers paid attention to OPSEC, it could have launched it as a successful envelopment or guerrilla operation.[13]

OPERATIONS

There is only one tactical principle which is not subject to change. It is to use the means at hand to inflict the maximum amount of wounds, death, and destruction on the enemy in the minimum amount of time.

—General George S. Patton, Jr.

The Operations Section (G3) is where planning, intelligence, manpower, communications, and logistics are translated into action. Some of the many G3's duties include:

1. Maintaining a current operation estimate of the situation and coordinating with other staff officers.

2. Recommending priorities for allocating critical resources of the command including time, personnel, supplies, and equipment.

3. Organizing and equipping units; estimating the numbers and types of units to be organized; and the priority for phasing in or replacing personnel and equipment in the units.

4. Preparing and carrying out training programs, directives, and orders. Plan and conduct field exercises.[14]

Operation *Desert Storm* is an example of an integrated operation called AirLand Battle Doctrine. Ground forces coordinate with air assets to produce mobile, mutually reinforcing combined-arms operation. For example, MLRS (Multiple Launched Rocket System) suppresses the enemy air defense systems allowing Air Force A-10s to neutralize enemy artillery and tanks behind the front line. As the air force destroys and suppresses the opposition, infantry and attack helicopters disrupt the enemy's rear areas. Engineer, armored, and mechanized infantry units supported by artillery and air strikes, breach enemy defensive lines and rendezvous with the airmobile infantry. J-STAR aircraft observe enemy troop movements and dispositions and relay information to air and ground commanders. AWACs aircraft keep a deep watch for enemy air act'vity. Air-superiority fights (F-15s) fly combat patrols and are ready to engage any enemy aircraft.[15]

The Navy launched Tomahawk cruise missiles at Iraqi high priority targets. Advanced Warning and Control Systems (AWACS) circled the skies transmitting phony radio messages to mislead the enemy. EF-111 carrying high powered transmitters jammed enemy air defense systems. F-117A Stealth fighters neutralized telecommunications centers, military command posts, and strategic military installations. B52 bombers pounded Iraqi positions.

On February 23, the U.S. 101st Airborne Division (Airmobile) began deep reconnaissance operations preparations for what would be the most extensive helicopter offensive since Vietnam. The 101st Airborne Division's mission was to cut off Iraqi forces to the east and disrupt any Iraqi operations in the Euphrates River Valley to the northwest of Kuwait.

Engineers driving armored bulldozers punched seventy-three gaps in the berms clearing paths for the 3rd Armored Cavalry Regiment (ACR). In less than twenty-four hours it was 125 kilometers into Iraq and had to wait for the rest of the 24th Mechanized Infantry Division to catch up. The 3rd ACR overran two airfields, and began picking up enemy prisoners of war (EPW). On February 27, after confronting sporadic Iraqi artillery, it completed its objective to obstruct Iraqi forces was stopped close enough to Basra to see the city's lights.

The 1st and 2nd Marine Divisions advanced on Iraqi defensive belts. Attacking on three axes, the marines breached extensive minefields, barbed-wire obstacles, and fire trenches. Quickly crossing the first barrier, they blasted the second barrier with artillery fire. Allied artillery responded. Both divisions began moving through the breach. The marines lost less than ten vehicles and suffered fewer than fifty casualties.

Iraqi artillery began to diminish. Iraqi soldiers began surrendering en masse when they saw their "impregnable" defenses so easily breached. The numerous Iraqi POWs who had to be processed and sent to the rear began to impede the rate of advance.

On February 24, the 1st Brigade, 2nd Armored Division, under the operational control of the Marines entered the breaches and became the Marine Corps' exploitation unit and was heavily reinforced with an USMC Light Armored Infantry (LAI) battalion. The Marines also provided an ANGLICO (Air and Naval Gunfire Coordinating) platoon and other support units. 1st Brigade moved west, trying to link up with Syrian or Egyptian forces who were trying to advance along the Marine Corps left flank.

Behind a shield of artillery fire, the USMC divisions marched north toward Kuwait International Airport and Kuwait City reporting thousands of Iraqi surrenders. East of the Marines, two Saudi Arabian armor and mechanized infantry task forces supported by U.S. battleship sixteen inch gunfire, launched a penetration attack up the coast north of Khafji.[16]

With the advance going so successfully, the Coalition Force command decided to throw a "left hook" deep into Iraqi territory. The 101st Airborne was helilifted toward the Tigris and Euphrates River to set up a forward base. The Iraqi Army in the Kuwait theatre of operations (KTO) was about to be cut off and killed; especially the Republican Guard, Iraq's elite fighting force.

J-STARS intelligence data showed that some of the Iraqi mechanized forces and Republican Guard were beginning to emerge out of their fortifications. Coalition air forces reacted swiftly. The U.S. 1st Infantry Division breached border minefields and crashed into southern Iraq, accompanied by the British 1st Armored Division. The 2nd ACR advanced west, bypassing the Iraqi defenses and immediately engaged Iraqi mechanized units. An intense conflict occurred at "73 Easting" with 2nd ACR's M1A1's tanks destroying Iraqi bunkers and armored forces.

The 24th Infantry Mechanized Infantry Division advanced to the Euphrates River covering 250 kilometers in twenty-four hours, bringing it into position to cut off all Iraqi units in the "Basra Pocket." It then confronted elements of a "large Iraqi infantry unit" and began a direct attack on the Euphrates, February 26. On February 27, the 24th Infantry's 1/64 Armor Battalion and 2/4 Cavalry reached the Euphrates. This was a record-breaking movement for a mechanized ground force in the twentieth century. The 24th Infantry Division had advanced 368 kilometers in 4 days, an average of 92 kilometers a day. The previous record was a Russian force advancing through Manchuria in 1945. It marched 820 kilometers in 10 days averaging 82 kilometers a day.[17]

The Tiger Brigade continued to advance toward its ultimate objective, the Mutla Ridge behind Kuwait City. In the Wadi al Batin area, 1st Cavalry Division moved south as the British slashed behind the two Iraqi infantry divisions facing the 1st Cavalry. The British overran the infantry division's rear area and crashed into Iraqi infantry mechanized units. The mechanized forces began to surrender.

The main effort of 7th Corps attacked the Republican Guard with the British 1st Armored Division slicing below the rest of the corps and assaulting dug-in Iraqi mechanized locations in Kuwait. By 6:00 p.m. on February 26, Coalition Forces had destroyed over twenty-one Iraqi divisions. At midnight, the 24th Mechanized Infantry Division had reached the Euphrates River, blocking the last major avenue of escape.

On February 27, the 7th Corps supported by the 18th Airborne Corps attacked the following units of the Republican Guard: Tawakalna Mech, Adnan, Nebuchadnezzar, Al Faw infantry divisions, Medina and Hammurabi armored divisions, and RGFC Special Forces Division supported by an Iraqi armored brigade near Basra. Air strikes completely demolished Tawakalna. The 2nd ACR and elements of the 1st U.S. Armored Division continued to pursue Tawakalna's retreating troops.

By February 27, the 1st Marine Division had also established a perimeter around Kuwait City International Airport and the 2nd Marine Division blocked escape routes on the west and north sides of Kuwait City. Nearly 40,000 Iraqi soldiers still tried to escape from Kuwait City. U.S. troops referred to the withdrawal as the "Great Bug Out."

Tiger Brigade, 2nd Armored Division, attacked across the Mutla Ridge overrunning the Ali Al Airfield and driving toward the coast road. The Tiger Brigade destroyed thirty-three Iraqi armored vehicles and captured the "Police Station" after a fierce battle that included a dismounted infantry assault. By noon, February 27, Coalition intelligence estimates estimated that the conflict had rendered thirty-three Iraqi armored divisions ineffective.

All of the armored units of 7th Corps began converging on the "Basra Pocket" pulverizing the Iraqi Divisions with air, artillery, and tanks. The 2nd Brigade, 1st Armored Division engaged units of the Medina and Hammurabi Republican Guards Armored Divisions. The 3rd Armored Division made a 200-kilometer march during the night and not one of its

320 M1A1 tanks broke down. The U.S. 1st Mechanized Infantry Division advanced on Safwan, Iraq. The Iraqi forces had been decimated; the ground war was over.[18]

Businesses must also coordinate operations in order to succeed. At Nucor, a steel manufacturer, each of the 21 plant managers is responsible for everything from sales to production to personnel. While it may be cheaper to centralize those functions at headquarters, the steelmaker figures the improved responsiveness to the marketplace outweighs the cost of duplication. Steelworkers are also eligible for productivity and quality bonuses that are typically 130% to 150% of their base pay. This gives workers pay of about $50,000 a year-approximately what unionized workers earn at other mills. However, Nucor's productivity is far higher. At its Crawfordsville, Indiana, plant; it takes less than one worker-hour to produce a ton of flat-rolled steel, compared with an average of four worker-hours elsewhere.[19]

In 1996, Apple had lost $1 billion on revenues of $7.1 billion. Steve Jobs, co-founder of Apple in 1975, returned as interim CEO in September 1997 and made changes in products, personnel, structure, marketing, manufacturing, and distribution.

Licensing. Jobs' first major move was to terminate the licensing agreements of several companies that had been manufacturing and selling Apple Macintosh clones. Executives now state 99% of customers who purchased the clones were already Mac users. Instead of expanding Apple's market, the clones were draining its profits.

Product Lines. Apple had also lost its focus trying to support 15 product lines. Jobs decided to halt production of Newtons and printers. He emphasized just four products: desktop and portable Macintoshes for consumers and professionals. The emphasis was on consumers, with the pro models targeting publishing and design customers.

Corporate structure. Apple's corporate structure had become too inefficient and decentralized. For example, it had 22 marketing groups throughout the company. Jobs created corporate-wide departments for manufacturing, marketing, sales, and finance.

Marketing. Jobs rehired Lee Clow, the TBWA Chiat/Day executive who created the ads for the original Macintosh. Clow and Jobs designed product and image ads the revived their impressive campaigns from the mid-1980s. The message: Buy a Macintosh and join an exclusive group of creative geniuses such as Albert Einstein, Miles Davis, and John Lennon, who "think different."

Distribution/Inventory. Jobs and sales chief Mitch Mandich determined they would sell Macintoshes only through stores that were committed to Apple, including the nations largest computer retailer, CompUSA. Thousands of indifferent outlets were removed. Jobs also brought in as operations chief Tim Cook, a Campaq Computer veteran known as "Attila the Hun of inventory." Cook reduced inventory from $400 million in December 1996 to $78 million as September 1998.[20]

Conversely, the case of Silicon Graphics, Inc. (SGI), shows what happens when operations are not coordinated. In 1994, *Business Week* called Silicon Graphics the "gee-whiz company." Its brilliant three-dimensional computer animated graphics created the ferocious Tyrannosaurus Rex and raptors of the movie *Jurassic Park*. Nintendo utilized the same technology to design a new generation of game machines with the quality of an arcade. Sales were climbing. For the fiscal year that ended June 30, 1995, revenue had soared 45% to 2.2 billion.[21]

While SGI dashed into new markets such as supercomputers, interactive cable TV, and digital film studios it neglected its core computer business. It also ignored such business basics as marketing, inventory management, and quality control. This produced machines that were late or incomplete. Engineering and production were split up among different groups, each section competing for resources. In addition, there was no coordination of schedules, overwhelming manufacturing. Poor planning often led to the company shipping 80% of its quarterly revenue in the last month of the quarter. "Things always got slammed into manufacturing in the last three weeks of the quarter," said a former manager. As a result, SGI's share of the 12.7 billion dollar workstation market fell from 14% in 1995 to 12% in the first quarter of 1997.[22]

Edward McCracken, CEO, decided it was time to develop a new agenda. He placed all computer engineering under the direction of Executive Vice-President Edward H. Ewald to achieve better coordination between research and development and manufacturing.

Silicon Graphics also improved its business processes such as demand forecasting and inventory management. One consideration SGI's previous demand forecasting model did not factor in was that many companies prefer to wait until new products have been in the market for some time. Many customers avoided the newer machines and kept buying the older ones resulting in a shortage of older models.

Despite McCracken's changes, SGI continued to lose money. In 1997, SGI posted a $56 million first quarter loss and McCracken resigned.

Operations Plans and Orders

Commanders use plans and orders to synchronize military actions. Plans and orders express to subordinates battlefield visualization, intent and decisions, focusing on the results the commander wants to achieve. A **plan** is a proposal for executing a command decision or project. Plans involve future operations, help the staff make assumptions about a situation, and are not static. As the situation changes, so does the plan.

A plan becomes an **order** when conditions of execution occur and an execution time is determined. An order is a written or oral communication directing action. The operations (OPORD) contains five paragraphs:

1. Situation—Describes the background surrounding the circumstances.
2. Mission—States what is to be accomplished.
3. Execution—How the mission is to be achieved.

4. Service Support—Describes the logistical support non-combat service support commanders will receive during their operation.
5. Command and Signal—Identifies the chain of command if not addressed in unit standard operating procedures (SOP). Lists signal instructions not specified in unit SOPs. Identifies specific signal additions in effect, required reports and formats, and the times reports are submitted.[23]

This format can easily be applied to business. Managers and supervisors can give a brief description of the situation and what needs to be done. They can tell their subordinates how the task is to be completed. Different departments can coordinate with each other to find out who is responsible for what assignments. Are the people on hand to accomplish the project? Has Production let Purchasing know what it needs to be procured? Has Sales and Marketing identified customers and competition. Can Shipping deliver the product on time? If problems arise, who can be contacted to get clarification about the situation?

Many business projects have failed because no one communicated with each other and no one knew what tasks and areas were their responsibility. A little communication and coordination increases the chances of a successful project.

LOGISTICS

I don't know much about this thing call logistics: All I know is that I want some.
—Expression, famous since World War I attributed to various American generals.

All armies need food, fuel, and ammunition. In addition, a modern army requires spare parts for vehicles, batteries for radios, weapons parts, clothing, tools, and building materials. These supplies must be delivered to the combat units in a constant flow in order to sustain an army's combat power.[24]

For example, during a rapid ground offensive a U.S. Army armor division will consume over 8,000 tons of supplies per day. The 16,000 troops, 320 M1A1 tanks, 210 Bradleys, 72 M109A3 self-propelled howitzers, and battery of Multiple Launch Rocket System (MLRS) will consume 1,800 tons of fuel, 1,000 tons of water, 5,000 tons of ammunition and use tons of spare parts. The troops will eat 48,000 meals.[25]

The G4 is the primary staff officer in the areas of supply, maintenance, transportation, and services. He maintains close and continuous coordination with the support command commander, who is responsible for logistical support, and the G3 for support of tactical operations.[26]

The Gulf War provides an excellent example of successful logistics. Although they were never really challenged, the Coalition Forces were able to move enormous amounts of soldiers and material quickly. From August 2, 1990, to January 17, 1991, the U.S. Transportation Command moved more than 500,000 people and 13 billion tons of equipment and supplies to the Middle East. Coalition Forces moved an average of 30,000 tons of supplies a day into Saudi Arabia.[27]

Major General William G. Pagonis, head of the Army's Central Support Command had to build a distribution system from scratch. By the end of the war, the network consisted of approximately 50,000 workers, 100,000 trucks, massive open-air warehouses, and had operating expenses near $1 billion.[28]

Business has also discovered the importance of logistics. Compaq Computer, a leading manufacturer of PCs estimates it lost $500 million to $1 billion in sales because its laptops and desktops weren't available where and when customers were ready to buy them. On average, only 40% of Compaq's computers reached the customers on time.[29]

Saturn has developed a sophisticated logistics system that links its suppliers, factories, and dealers together. Saturn maintains almost no component inventory. Its suppliers, located in 39 states, deliver pre-inspected and presorted parts at precise times to the factory's 56 receiving docks, 21 hours a day, six days a week. A central computer-directs the trucks to the proper receiving dock.[30]

Wal-Mart has also developed a concept called integrated logistics. It uses an electronic data interchange system to transmit daily sales information to suppliers. The suppliers' computers integrate this information with warehouse inventory information and sales projections to generate a new order. In addition, Wal-Mart also utilizes flow-through or one-stop logistics to streamline its distribution network. Two sets of trucks, one from the vendors' factories and one heading to the stores arrive simultaneously at a company loading dock. Workers move the product from the first set of trucks into the second set of trucks. The product then proceeds to its final destination avoiding any warehouse storage.[31]

In the late 1980's, General Electric Appliances designed the Direct Connect Program to help recast itself into a economical, no-headache supplier to retailers.

The Direct Connect System gives dealers access to GE's on-line order-processing system 24 hours a day. Retailers can check model availability and place orders for next day delivery. Dealers receive GE's best price regardless of order size. In addition, Direct Connect retailers also receive priority over other dealers in delivery scheduling and consumer financing through GE Credit with the first 90 days free of interest.

In exchange, Direct Connect distributors agree to sell nine major GE product categories while stocking only carryout products such as microwave ovens and air conditioners ensuring that GE products generate 50 percent of sales. They also agree to open their books for review and to pay GE through electronic funds transfer on the 25th day of the month after purchase.

While retailers have had to give up some of their float time in payables, the accessibility of having their own back-room inventory, and some independence from the supplier, they receive GE's best prices while eliminating the inconvenience and cost of maintaining inventory. As a result, their profit margins on GE products have jumped.

General Electric gets half of the retailer's business and saves about 12 percent of distribution and marketing costs. GE also saves time and labor in responding to inquiries and in order entry since dealers serve themselves through the network. In addition, GE can track consumer sales because it knows that orders are actual sales, not requests for additional inventory. It has integrated its order entry system to other systems involved in forecasting demand, planning production, and distribution. This allows the company to manufacture in response to customer demand instead of inventory. Instead of a maintaining a complex and expensive distribution system the company has 10 strategically located warehouses that can deliver appliances to 90 percent of the country within 24 hours.[32]

Logistics used to be a neglected area of business. However, many companies are reexamining and improving their logistics operations and increasing profits. Without an adequate supply of raw materials and a capable distribution system a company cannot compete effectively in today's market.

6. Deception

All warfare is based on deception

—Sun Tzu

Deception is as old as warfare. King Thutmose III (reigned 1504-1450 B.C.) used a ruse to capture the city of Jaffa (known as Yafo in modern Israel). Captain Thut, in Thutomosels service, took two hundred soldiers and embarked by ship to Jaffa while the royal army marched up the coast. When the ship neared Jaffa, some of the men were sewn into the large sacks normally used for grain. When the ship docked, the "crew" of the ship began unloading the cargo while the "captain", Thut paid the port duties. That night Thut's commandos disrupted the defender's rear. Thutmosels army stormed the city and Jaffa fell.[1]

We in the West view deception in an unfavorable light. However, in other parts of the world, such as Asia or the Middle East, skill at military and political deception is regarded as an admirable talent and a more humane alternative to armed combat.

One of the more successful architects of deception in European history were the Byzantines. They kept their half of the Roman Empire running for another thousand years after the city of Rome fell in the fifth century. Often surrounded and outnumbered by more powerful opponents, the Byzantines learned that the enemy could be subdued without bloodshed. War was a last resort and should be used sparingly.

Deception was incorporated into standard army manuals such as *Tactica*, written by Emperor Leo the VI who reigned from 886 to 912. In addition to tactics like night attacks, ambushes, and surprise attacks, Leo suggested using some of the following techniques:

Bribing important officers in the opposition's army to throw a battle. During this period, many military leaders were mercenaries and susceptible to a better offer. Even commanders who were not mercenaries could be bought with gold or other favors. Since Byzantine intelligence and diplomatic services knew who was who in the foreign armies, they were able to determine the proper time to make the offer. As recently as the 1979-1988 Afghan War, the Soviets were able to bribe several Afghan tribal chiefs to stay out the fighting. It should also be noted the Russians consider themselves heirs to the Byzantines.

Circulating false reports of distant victories to bolster the morale of one's own men or reduce it of the enemy. Communications during this time were poor and the ability to compose and deliver a false message was more important than whether it was true or not. The Byzantines had skilled forgers and writing experts who could create convincing false messages. During the 1982 Falklands War, the British used this technique against the Argentines. When the British sent one of their feared Ghurka battalions to the Falklands, they made sure the Argentine defenders knew these knife-wielding Ghurkas were coming. This had the desired effect of reducing Argentine morale even further.

Another strategy the Byzantines used was engaging in protracted negotiations with the enemy, even when all hope of peace had disappeared, in order to gain time. This strategy is being used throughout the world today; from Bosnia to Iraq to North Korea.

Composing treasonable letters from important officers in the enemy's army, and making sure their commander accidentally got a hold of them. Again, the Byazantine skill at forgery and their superior

intelligence gathering ability enabled them to create convincing decep-
tions. As the implements of forgery have improved, this form of deception has become more common in the Twentieth Century. It was used
during the Cold War and is still used today.[2]

During the Gulf War, the Coalition Forces conducted deception operations before invading the Iraqis western flank. A radio deception plan,
consisting of radio operators generating a lot of radio traffic depicting
several divisions preparing to advance, was implemented.[3] The United
States lst Cavalry Division made many aggressive raids near southern
border of Kuwait prior to the beginning of the ground offensive. The lst
Cavalry's tanks and mechanized infantry drove straight at Iraqi positions
to convince the Iraqis that the American forces were going to attack
frontally, as the Iranians had done during the 1980-88 war.[4]

Meanwhile, the U.S. Marine Corps and U.S. Navy rehearsed for an
amphibious assault into Kuwait. Although the invasion was never executed, it succeeded in displacing six Iraqi divisions guarding the coast.[5]

Businesses may also use deception. Chin-Ning Chu, author of *Thick
Face, Black Heart*, took on an Oregon grass seed company who wanted
to sell grass seed to mainland China, as one of her clients in 1986.
However, the Chinese considered grass a weed and did not plant it for-
ornamental purposes. The Chinese idea of beautification was to pull
grass out, not to plant it.

Chu approached the Chinese government telling them her client
wanted to buy grass seed and was looking for a low-cost producer. The
Chinese could produce the seeds and then sell them back to the
Americans and earn foreign currency. Since Chinese officials often view
foreigners as unsophisticated, Chu portrayed her American client as
naive and her proposal was accepted.

However, Chu knew the weather conditions and agricultural methods in China would not support grass production at a reasonable cost.
She began to visit China. Accompanied by American technicians, she

taught the Chinese the production skills, the benefits of grass seed, and how to maintain a lush emerald lawn.

A few years later, the Chinese stopped producing American grass seed because it was too expensive. However, they had learned the value of American grass seed and began to buy it from her client. In 1990, China hosted the Asian Olympic Games and the fields were covered with American grass.

After the Asian Olympic Games, American grass seed was planted in Bejing's royal gardens, currently the home and office of China's highest official, Deng Xiapong and Jiang Zemin, the secretary general of the Chinese Communist Party.[5]

The specialty beer market has been growing at more than 40% annual rate. In an effort to capitalize on this growth, Miller Brewing and Anheuser-Busch have attempted to enter the market. However, in doing so, both breweries have avoided prominently displaying their name.

Borrowing a marketing strategy used by such companies as Hallmark (Shoebox Greetings) and General Motors Corporation (Saturn) the large brewers are trying to think and act small. Miller Brewing Company, for instance, resurrected the 19th century Plank Road Brewery to produce its Icehouse and Red Dog Beers. It also set up Specialty/Craft Company to direct its 1988 acquisitions of Celis and Jacob Leinenkugal.

Anheuser-Busch bought 25% of Seattle's Redhook Ale Brewery. It also converted a 15 barrel test brewery in St. Louis to create new brews such as Elk Mountain Amber Ale and Crossroads Beer. Coors built the Sandlot Brewery, located at the new Coors Field baseball park in Denver, Colorado, to develop new products.

Initial reaction to these deception operations has been mixed. Christopher Finch, co-author or America's Best Beers, calls Red Dog Beer "totally uninteresting" and rates Elk Mountain Amber Ale a two out of five on his scale, "if I was being generous." Christopher Ruderman, an ordinary microbeer drinker says of Miller's Red Dog Beer "it doesn't impress me in the slightest." As for Anheuser-Busch's Red Wolf promotion, "I ain't buying."[7]

Time will tell if business will become as adept at deception as the Byzantines.

7. Leadership

You don't manage people; you manage things.
You lead people.
—Grace Hopper, U.S. Navy Admiral, retired

Staff Sergeant (SSG) Roy Benavidez woke on the morning of May 2, 1968, and saw helicopter pilots scrambling around the Forward Operating Base in Loc Ninh, Vietnam. The radio's airwaves were filled with the shouts of men requesting an immediate evacuation from their position deep behind enemy lines.

He sprinted to the nearest evacuation helicopter preparing for take-off. Armed with only and 18-inch knife strapped to his side, Benavidez jumped aboard, strapped himself in, and said "Take me with you." The chopper pilots shook their heads in disbelief. They had never seen a crazier-or more suicidal—sergeant.

The helicopter dropped Benavidez off at the landing zone a few hundred feet from the surviving members of the Special Forces patrol. Within seconds of his rescue mission, he received the first of many wounds. "As soon as I hit the ground I felt something like a thorn stinging my leg," he recalled. When he reached down and felt his calf, his fingers were coated with blood.

While the North Vietnamese Army (NVA) saturated the air with a storm of bullets, hand grenades, mortar rounds, Benavidez crawled to the team's position, patched their wounds and shifted them into better fighting positions. Meanwhile, another AK-47 round ripped through his thigh and shrapnel tore his face and head. He clenched his teeth and urged the men to hold on until the helicopters circled to pick them up.

When the choppers touched down in a nearby clearing, Benavidez made several trips carrying his comrades through a storm of bullets. When the last of the living soldiers were on the helicopter, he realized the team's classified documents were still with the corpse of the team leader—material he didn't dare permit to fall into enemy hands. As he dragged the team leader's body back to the hovering helicopter, another round struck Benavidez in the back and exiting below his armpit and missing his heart by millimeters. He passed out from the intense pain.

"When I regained consciousness, there was black smoke all over the clearing," he said. The helicopter, already seriously damaged from enemy fire, had crashed while waiting for the classified documents to be recovered. Under increasing weapons and grenade fire, Benavidez helped get everyone out of the chopper and back into another defensive perimeter. He then called for more helicopters to be sent from Loc Ninh and for tactical airstrikes to slow the advancing North Vietnamese Army. Moving among the men, he distributed water and ammunition and tried to sustain their spirits. Two more bullets struck Benavidez in the leg.

When he heard the extraction helicopter overhead he shouted to the other soldiers "Okay, let's go! We don't have permission to die here!" With the help of a newly arrived medic, Benavidez started ferrying his fellow soldiers to the helicopter. On his second trip, an NVA soldier crouched in the tall grass rose up and clubbed him from behind with the butt of his rifle. As Benavidez wheeled around to face his opponent, NVA solider sent another blow crashing into his jaw. The two fell to the ground and his foe started stabbing Benavidez's arm with his bayonet. The American reached for the one weapon he'd originally brought on the rescue mission and left it sticking out of his adversary's body.

During that rescue mission, Benavidez had suffered 35 bullet, shrapnel, and bayonet wounds. Weak and semi-conscious, the 32-year-old staff sergeant looked like just another corpse to the medic who had placed him in a body bag. Benavidez heard the zipper of the body bag closing over him but he was too weak to make any noise. He couldn't even blink his eyes. If it hadn't been for an alert sergeant who had noticed Benavidez in the stack of bodies off-loaded from the evacuation aircraft, he might have suffocated in the rubber bag. For his actions, Benavidez received the Congressional Medal of Honor, the nation's highest military award.[1]

Most leadership actions do not require such valiant measures. Field Manual (FM) 22-100 *Military Leadership* defines leadership as "influencing people—by providing purpose, direction, and motivation—while operating to accomplish the mission and improving the organization."[2]

Stuart R. Levine, CEO, and Michael A. Crom, VP, of Dale Carnegie & Associates define leadership "to help people achieve what they are capable of, to establish a vision for the future, to encourage, to coach and to mentor, and to establish and maintain successful relationships."[3].

William A. Cohen, author of *The Art of the Leader*, defines leadership as "the art of influencing others to their maximum performance to accomplish any task, objective, or project.[4]

The Armed Forces Officer, a manual on leadership written for officers in all our armed forces says "Though it has been said before, it can be said again: It is a paramount and overriding responsibility of every officer to take care of his men before caring for himself. It is a cardinal principle!"[5]

Hyrum W. Smith, CEO of the Franklin Quest Company, was once a platoon commander of a Pershing missile unit in Germany. When he took over command, morale was low. The unit was supposed to be able to mobilize in two hours. When Smith first arrived he guessed it would probably take three days for the unit to mobilize.

While in the field, the soldiers performing guard duty had to stand at their posts in temperatures often below zero without any shelter. Smith wanted to build some guard shacks for them. However, because there was so much else to do, there were no enlisted people to build the guard shacks. When he suggested that they build some shelters for the guards, one of the sergeants looked a him and said, "What do you mean, we?"

"Yeah, let's go build them," replied Smith.

"It's ten below zero out there."

"I don't care how cold it is. Let's go build them."

Smith dragged the officers and sergeants out and began building. They got some telephone poles, cut them off, put them in the ground, and built the first shack. They put a little heater and some insulation in the shack to keep out the cold. About two in the morning they put the first guards in the shack, and they were amazed these officers and non-commissioned officers were building shelters for them. By six o'clock the next night all the guards were standing in guard shacks, warm and dry.

Word quickly spread through the unit and morale began to immediately turn around. The guards began looking for things to do, and the unit reduced their firing times to about six and a half minutes. The unit also improved its mobilization time to 45 minutes.[6]

Smith realized a leader gets people to do things because they want to, not because they have to. Smith sent the message that the people at the top cared for the people at the bottom of the military hierarchy when he built those guard shacks. He was willing to get physically involved in doing something for them, and they then decided to return the favor. If you take care of the people below you, they'll take care of you. Your success is dependent on the people below you.

Mike Walsh, CEO of Union Pacific Railroad (UPRR) from 1986 to 1991 had been at his new job for about four months when he had heard that UPRR had made a drug raid in Louisiana. Management had called together maintenance and way workers under the guise of a safety meeting. When they arrived, they flattened the workers on the ground and used dogs to sniff for marijuana and cocaine. They didn't find anything. Walsh was outraged.

He told his people, "OK, I am personally getting on an airplane and so are you Mr. Head of Operations, and so are you, Mr. Head of Engineering. And we're going down there. We're going to meet with those people and apologize publicly to for what we did. We're going to tell them that we don't tolerate drugs in this railroad, but we don't tolerate this kind of management behavior either."

Walsh's staff was dumbfounded. They told him "you can't do that."

"Why the hell can't I?" Walsh replied. "Furthermore, I'm not going to do it. You're going with me."

Walsh and his staff flew to Louisiana and met with the workers. They accepted their apology in about ten minutes. Then Walsh asked, "You got anything else on your mind?" A worker raised his hand and said "You talk a lot about safety. Have you ever seen the bunk cars where we live? You don't have adequate safety precautions. The steps are a mess. If we have to get up in the middle of the night and go to the bathroom, we're going to get hurt."

One of Walsh's managers began to tell this worker how much money UPRR had spent on the maintenance of bunk cars each year. Walsh stopped him and said, "Look, that's got nothing to do with this guy's question. He said the bunk cars where he lives are unsafe. How far away are they?"

"About three blocks," answered the employee.

"Let's go take a look at them," said Walsh.

"But its pouring rain," replied the worker.

"We don't melt," responded Walsh. They went over to the bunk cars and they were exactly like the worker described—unsafe.

"Going down there said a lot to our people," recalls Walsh. "It said were are not going to tolerate the sort of behavior that was reflected in the drug raid. And it doesn't matter how much we spend each year—if somebody tells us that something is unsafe, we want to respond to that guy. We don't want to give him a lecture."[7]

Is there a difference between military and corporate leadership? Not according to General Fredrick J. Kroesen. General Kroesen fought in World War II, Korea, and Vietnam. During his military career, he progressed from second lieutenant to four-star general as Commander-in-Chief, Central Army Group of NATO. He has also worked with corporations and other organizations on an assortment of management and defense issues. During a meeting someone asked him about differences between leadership in the military and corporations. "The principles of leadership aren't different," replied Kroesen. "Where you have a successful leader, you have a successful corporation."[8]

William A. Cohen, author of *The Art of the Leader* outlines six actions you can take to help you be a successful leader:

actions to enhance leadership

1. Be willing to Take Risks
2. Be Innovative
3. Take Charge
4. Have High Expectations
5. Maintain a positive attitude
6. Get Out in Front[9]

Be Willing to Take Risks

R.W. Johnson, Jr., former CEO of Johnson & Johnson said, "Failure is our most important product." Johnson & Johnson's philosophy is Throughout its history, has had numerous failures. Its experiment with colored casts for children was abandoned because the food dyes turned bed linens into a collage of colors and hospital laundries into chaos. More recently, it has had failed endeavors in heart valves, kidney dialysis machines, and ibuprofen pain relievers.[10]

However, along with those setbacks, Johnson & Johnson has had many successes. Among those successes are Johnson's Baby Powder and the Band-Aid. In 1890, Johnson & Johnson received a letter from a physician who complained about patient skin irritation from certain medicated plasters. Fred Kilmer, director of research, sent him a packet of assuasive Italian talc to apply on the skin. He then persuaded the company to include a small can of talc with certain products. To the J&J's amazement, patrons began requesting more of the talc. The company responded by creating "Johnson's Toilet and Baby Powder," which became a famous household product around the world.[11]

In 1920, J&J employee Earle Dickson devised a ready-made bandage for his wife who had a habit of cutting herself with kitchen knives. When he mentioned his design to the marketing people they decided to test the product on the market. After a slow start and endless tinkering, Band-Aid products became the biggest selling category in the company's history.[12]

Take Charge

Several years ago a small southern California aerospace firm of 350 employees made oxygen masks and other life-support equipment for military and civilian pilots. The company's primary competitor was another small firm on the East Coast. Both companies competed heavily for the same government contracts in numerous areas.

During an exceptionally fierce competition the West Coast company ran into deep financial difficulty. One reason was the higher salaries on the West Coast. But the biggest issue was that everyone had a "business as usual" attitude. From manager to worker, they did their jobs. If the company was in trouble, that was someone else's problem. They thought they were doing the best they possibly could.

Suddenly, the company ran out of money. With no cash reserves, it could not manufacture any goods. It could not meet payrolls. To complicate the situation, the president of the company committed suicide. The firm went into Chapter 11 bankruptcy, where the bank takes control of the company to try and save it.

The bank sought an experienced person who could lead the company out of trouble. That person was Aaron Bloom. He had previously been a vice-president of engineering with the company and had left several years earlier.

Bloom took charge of the company. He gathered the remaining fifty employees and made an announcement. "From eight in the morning until five in the afternoon, we'll all perform our regular duties. If you are a secretary, you will do secretarial work. If you're a manager, you'll manage. If you are a design engineer, you'll design. After five o'clock, everyone, from the secretaries to myself will help the production line put the product together. You and I will take our orders from the production supervisors. There will be no pay for this, but there will be sandwiches for supper."

Bloom answered questions and then concluded: "We are going to return this company to its rightful place of saving live by supplying a quality product at a good price. We are also going to save our jobs. I know we can do this. If I thought we couldn't, I wouldn't be here."

Within two years, this small aerospace company had proceeded to return to its previous position. The firm hired more workers and was again profitable.

Cohen notes that everyone worked hard to turn the company around and they did so without compensation. He asks the questions: Why didn't they do this before they went into Chapter 11? Had they done so, they would have run out of money and no one would have been fired. Why didn't they do this? Why was it necessary to sacrifice 300 employees of the company before this happened. And how could it be that 50 people could do more than 350 had done?

Cohen speculates that the 350 workers felt they could not make a difference nor did they care. Aaron Bloom made them see that they could do it and made them care.[13]

Have High Expectations

James Belasco ran a specialty chemical facility. Although the plant was among the leaders in its segment, it still dumped 5 percent of its product due to poor quality. At least a dozen times a month the facility was taking back product from customers because it didn't meet specifications.

Belasco was worried. How many times would a customer reorder after sending back a bad batch? How many precious dollars were they spilling down the drain every day? How long before someone started to lean on them about where they put their toxic waste? How long before someone figured out how to lose only 1 percent and priced them out of the business?

Belasco realized he had to get the plant to focus achieving a zero percent waste. He came to the plant the next day and asked the employees, "What will it take to make perfect product? What will it take to dump not a drop of bad product down the drain?" At first, the employees said it couldn't be done. Then one technician said, "We could do this, and that, and…" Four weeks later, after rearranging the line and changing several procedures, the plant had its first perfect day.[14]

Maintain a Positive Attitude

To work at Nordstrom's, a positive attitude is mandatory. "When people shop at Nordstrom, they deserve the best attitude," explained Bill, a five year veteran. "I always have my smile, for anybody, everybody." Nordstrom's customer service is legendary. The Nordie who ironed a new shirt for a customer who needed it for a meeting that afternoon. The Nordie who cheerfully gift-wrapped products. The Nordie who warmed customers' cars in the winter while the customers finished shopping; the Nordie who made a last minute delivery of party clothes to a harried party hostess; and the Nordie who refunded money for a set of tire chains-although Nordstrom doesn't sell tire chains.

There are also tales of Nordstrom salespersons being sent home early for getting irritated with a customer or salespersons being reprimanded for frowning.[15]

Get Out in Front

The Israeli Army requires it officers to be first when leading troops. This is counter to the doctrine taught in the U.S. Army and other armed forces around the world. Most armies teach that to effectively direct the troops, the commander should be with a forward unit, but not the most forward. If he is leading a patrol, he can be the number two soldier, but not the first. If he is not at the front he won't know what's going on. However, if he is all the way up front he is more like to become a casualty. This results in a higher casualty rate for officers, often a scarce asset.

The Israelis ignore this premise and tell their officers: "If you are an officer, that's what you get paid for. You have to been in front of your men." They have done this in every war they have fought and as a consequence have the highest officer casualty rate in the world. Despite this statistic they do it anyway because they understand that leaders must lead by getting out in front.[16]

The Marine Corps also stresses commanding from a forward position. In every war, Marine Corps officers have suffered a higher casualty rate than their counterparts in the army infantry. The Marine Corps officer wants to observe what the enemy is planning to do. He wants real time information.

Business managers must also learn to lead from forward position. The more important the assignment, the more important it is to be at the front. In the forward position a manager can see for himself the difficulties of accomplishing his directions. He also has real-time information and can make immediate decisions. A manager who spent time on the front line is able to give his superiors honest appraisals rather than what they want to hear.[17]

At the Dayton-Hudson Corporation, every major executive takes the escalator to their ninth floor offices; a tradition started by Don Dayton. Dayton recognized that the best business information was not found in a business report or other second hand information. It was steady, immediate unfiltered information from employees and customers.[18]

Tom Peters, author of *Thriving on Chaos,* calls getting out in front "visible management." Here are his ten recommendations for implementing visible management:

Put on a note card in your pocket and write on it: "Remember, I'm out here to listen." Listening to your subordinates provides you with feedback from the people on the receiving end of your leadership. Listen and learn.

Take notes and provide feedback. Listen and take notes. Note taking lets other persons know you are taking their comments seriously. Fix minor items immediately or within twenty-four hours. It doesn't have to be a major item. A directive eliminating an asinine regulation; or a faulty toilet is fixed in a couple of hours; or having new equipment installed in the plant within a few weeks.

Cycle your actions through the chain of command. Take direct action on some of the minor issues. However, notify your chain of command and let them handle and take credit for the majority of your follow-up actions.

Protect informants. As your commitment to listening and mending things becomes evident, you hear less and less sugarcoated versions of truth, often passing through informal channels. Use these channels with care and make sure that no informant gets burned by an enraged supervisor. And if a supervisor reprimands a person who was frank with you about a problem, remove him or her from managerial responsibility immediately.

Be patient. When you first begin to roam around and check out areas, you will be treated cautiously. Often, you are threatening an established practice of comfortable, if unproductive, non-communication. Only time and repetition will lead to persons feeling comfortable speaking with you. Only your repeated instances of prompt follow-up and action will make it worth their time to talk voluntarily.

Listen, but preach a little too. Don't give a sermon; use small, specific episodes related to housekeeping or excessive paperwork to reinforce your principle theme. If the requisition of a part requires three signatures, declare the form dead. Then check next week to make sure the form died—or that the procedures were at least streamlined.

Don't give much advance notice and travel alone. Giving limited advance notice is not meant to surprise people, it is meant to evade the truth-inhibiting embellishments prepared for visits from "corporate headquarters". Whatever your management level, don't bring an entourage with you. Take your own notes.

Work some night shifts and take a basic training course.

In the book *Company Command, The Bottom Line,* by John G. Meyer Jr., General John A. Wickham, Jr., Army Chief of Staff, 1985-1988, told the following story: When he graduated from West Point in 1950, he was assigned to a weapons platoon in Europe. The platoon had an array of weapons including 57mm recoiless rifles and 60mm mortars. Wickham did not know anything about these weapons.

However, he had an outstanding platoon sergeant—Sergeant First Class (SFC) Putnam. SFC Putnam asked him if he would like to learn the weapons crew drill to learn more about the weapons. Wickham jumped at the opportunity. His unit was training in Grafenwohr, Germany. For the next ten days, after supper, SFC Putnam Lieutenant (LT) Wickham to a muddy spot next to the latrine for weapons training.

At first, LT Wickham couldn't figure out why Putnam had chosen this spot for training, but he soon learned why. After supper, every soldier in the unit usually visited the latrine and inevitably looked over the screen and saw their platoon sergeant teaching the new lieutenant the crew drill. The soldiers immediately knew *their* lieutenant cared and was willing learn from *their* platoon sergeant. Like LT Wickham, take advantage of anyone, regardless of rank, who can teach you how to do your job better. Don't be too overconfident or arrogant.[19]

Beware of the subtle demands you put on your subordinates that prevent them from practicing visible management.

You may exhort your people to get out but then you call them for some information you need immediately. You have just sent the message: "Getting out is great, but be in the office whenever I beckon." Say good-bye to visible management.

Use routines to force yourself and your colleagues to get out. Ask questions that can't be answered without firsthand knowledge. Develop or assign projects that can't be done at a desk.[20]

8. Training

The difference between a rabble and an effective professional Army is training. No task is more important than training.

—General E.C. Meyer

In the military, training to fight to win is a commander's most important responsibility. There a three levels of training: training for individual soldiers, collective training for the unit, and training for unit leaders.[1]

The G3 is the person concerned with training. His responsibilities include:

—Identifying training requirements based on combat and garrison missions.

—Preparing and executing training programs, directives, and orders.

—Planning and conducting field exercises.

—Determining requirements for and the allocation of training resources. This includes ammunition for training, acquiring ranges and facilities, and training aids.

—Organizing and conducting internal schools. Obtaining and allocating quotas for external schools.[2]

Military personnel are constantly receiving both formal and informal training. Typically, an enlisted person attends Basic Training, a

Military Occupational School (MOS), and Noncommissioned Officer Courses.

Officers attend a military academy, a Reserve Officer Training Course (ROTC), West Point, or Officer Candidate School (OCS); Officer Basic Course, Officer Advanced Course, Combined Arms Staff Service School, and the Command and General Staff Course.

Businesses must also pay attention to training. According to Forbes magazine:

> America is standing tall again militarily because we heavily invested in a highly trained force and advanced technology. The reason America is having trouble economically is that we neither invest in a highly trained work force nor devote adequate resources to advanced civilian technology, nor take a systematic approach to our economic strategy.[3]

Successful businesses realize the importance of training. Motorola, for example, spends approximately 4% of its payroll cost on training and development compared with an average of 1.2% for all U.S. companies. A typical Motorola employee receives 40 hours of training areas such as teamwork and problem solving. Employees may also take communications and technical courses or can attend classes at Motorola University in Schaumburg, Illinois. This training has paid off in the form of improved quality of work. Motorola calculates it has reduced defects from 7,000 defects for every one million opportunities to make mistakes in 1987 to 30 defects in 1995.[4]

In the military, the cost of poor training is death or injury. In business, ineffective training affects the bottom line.

What Training Can Do

1. *It can significantly improve individuals' skills making them more competent at their jobs.* Mazda spent approximately $11,000 to train

each worker it hired for its new plant in Flat Rock, Michigan, *before* it opened the plant.

2. *It can provide workers with clear expectations of quality, quantity and timeliness.* It is able to inform workers of company policies and procedures that are meaningful to them. It helps employees set realistic priorities. It can assist them comprehend their positions in the organization, choose where to go for help with a dilemma and appreciate the final product they help create will be utilized.

What Training Will Not Do

1. *It will not improve the means available to do the job.* In fact, insufficient support systems increase necessary training. For example, each year training organizations contracted to train all types of data entry personnel. Why? Many times the automated system doesn't have clear, concise, and easy to understand procedures for entering data. Worse, the automated system itself causes the errors. No amount of training will correct this problem.

2. *It will not reliably motivate workers.* This one of the most frequent misuses of training. A person's motivations is the result of all performance factors and their need structure. Many companies have training to motivate managers as well as workers. Workers attend the training and get motivated. However, two weeks later, everything is the same as it was before.

3. *It will not provide a substitute for useful feedback.* Feedback is essential for improving performance. If employees don't get feedback on how effectively they are applying the training, even the best training will fail.

Three Points to Remember

1. The primary purpose of training is the maximum amount of learning for the minimum amount of money.

2. The objective of this learning is improved performance.

3. Workers' performance depends on what makes sense to them to do in certain circumstances. What makes sense is based on what workers know and knowing how to do it, having the resources to do it, their motivation to do, and the feedback they receive. Enhancing their performance requires changing one or more of these conditions so that improved performance is what makes sense to them. Employees won't use anything they receive in training unless it's supported and reinforced back on the job.[5]

Dan Carrison and Rod Walsh authors of the book *Semper Fi, Business Leadership the Marine Corps Way* write:

> How many corporations can truly say their training programs are run by the best the company can offer? All too often, corporate trainers are veteran employees the company doesn't quite know what else to do with. They are not "trained to be trainers," and many are not particularly proud of what they do. There is no master plan to ensure every new hire receives an identical indoctrination, so instructors end up teaching *their* way, perpetuating a culture that may or may not be in the best interest of the corporation.[6]

Some corporations, such as the Walt Disney Company, Nordstrom, and IBM do indoctrinate. Disney requires every new employee to attend a new employee orientation known as "Disney Traditions". Faculty of Disney University, the company's internal and socialization and training organization teach the course designed a course designed to give new members an introduction to its traditions, philosophies, organization and the way Disney does business.[7]

Training is also continuous at successful corporations. At FedEx individual development and extensive training are emphasized. FedEx spends 3% of total expenses on training, six times the ratio at other companies. Thousands of employees from couriers to top executives have attended the Leadership Institute near Memphis, Tennessee. During their first year, front line and second level managers must attend 10 to 11 weeks of mandatory training.[8]

Here's a condensed training list:
1. Establish the supervisor as the corporate teacher.
2. Require and support continuing education.
3. Ensure that every manager is entitled to lead.
4. Prepare your subordinates for two jobs—theirs and yours.
5. Be a teacher, not a boss.[9]

9. Women in the Workplace and the Military

There is still a very issue of acceptance. We talk about sexual harassment, we talk about these things, but to me they're all symptoms. To me the illness is basic acceptance.
—Marine Brigadier General Gail Reals speaking at her retirement.

Once upon a time…strong, independent women were call witches and were burned at the stake…Today they're called feminists…they publish web pages, get flamed in e-mail and are blamed for most of society's problems…its not perfect…but its a lot better than the stake.
—Caption from the website gendergap.com.

Before we discuss how the military and business are alike, let's look how they are different. One area the military is different is pay. A woman receives the same pay as her male counterparts.

This is not always the case in the civilian sector. According to Catalyst, a research organization that works to advance women the business, women managers earn from 48 cents to 67 cents for every dollar paid to a white male manager. Asian women managers earn 67 cents, white women earn 59 cents, black women earn 58 cents and Hispanic women earn 48 cents. Male minority managers earn 73 cents of that dollar. All categories of women earn less than men in their same ethnic groupings.[1]

According to Department of Labor Statistics, for the first quarter of 1998, women earned 76 cents for every dollar men made compared to 73 cents during the same period of 1997.[2]

However, the number of women owned businesses is increasing. In 1999, there were 8.5 million female-owned businesses, more than a third of all U.S. businesses. Between 1987 and 1997 their total sales grew 161 percent and their work forces grew 262 percent.[3]

America's workplace demographics are changing. According to the Bureau of Labor Statistics, more women are becoming the family's primary breadwinner. Of the 54 million households with married couples, 5.5 percent rely on the wife to bring home the bulk of the income. Furthermore, in duel-income families, 22 percent of wives earn more than their husbands, up from 18 percent in 1987 and 4.4 percent in 1970.[4]

In the military, the demographics are also changing. In 1997, Major General Claudia J. Kennedy became Deputy Chief of Staff for Intelligence and the Army's first female three-star general.[5] Brigadier General Sue Dueitt is the female Reserve general officer not the Army Nurse Corps. Her assignment in 1997 was Deputy Chief for Public Affairs, Headquarters, Department of the Army.[6] Maj. Gen. Celia L. Adolphi became the first two-star general in the history of the Army Reserve.[7]

Critics of military policies would probably state that it's about time. They would argue that it took over 220 years for women to be promoted into top jobs. There is also the issue of the combat exclusion rule.

It's interesting to watch the two sides debate each other. Both use spokeswomen and both claim to be acting in the interest of women. Elaine Donnelly, spokeswoman for the Center for Military Readiness, an organization which opposed gender integration, stated: "Gender integration has gone far beyond the military's scope and mission, and in the process it has injured women and reduced the challenges of men. This report may force people to get over their fear of feminists and look seriously at the military's moral problems—coed tents in Bosnia, too many pregnancies on Navy ships and sexuality out of control in the barracks."[8]

Rosemary Mariner, a retired Navy captain said "This overreaction is not being driven as much by concern for military readiness as by social conservatives pushing an anti-woman agenda. They pit soldier against soldier and try to make us forget that the reason we have women in the military is because we need them."[9]

Here's one argument stating why women should not be allowed in combat:

> Warriors kill. If someone cannot kill, regardless of the reason(s), that individual is not a warrior. Men make the best warriors in comparison to women because men are better at killing in war.
>
> Women cannot compete on the battlefield as they cannot compete in professional sports. Women do not hold even one Olympic world record for strength or speed. Women are weaker and slower on average as well.
>
> Strength, not weakness wins battles and wars.
>
> Add to these undeniable physiological facts and the effects of socialization of women in American society and a simple fact becomes clearly evident to all but the most confused and misguided—women are no better suited to win wars than men are suited to have babies.
>
> Women who claim the title of soldier, sailor, airman, or marine bring to mind an old saying—'you can paint black stripes on a white horse and call it a zebra but that doesn't make it one.[10]

For those who feel that women should not be in combat, they should check the history books. In 1429, the city of Orléans, France, had been under siege for seven months. The English had encircled most of the city with forts. Earlier, the French had suffered a devastating defeat at the "Battle of Herrings" when they failed to prevent reinforcements from reaching the English forts surrounding Orléans. Only through the Burgundy Gate on the east side of the city could food and supplies be brought in. The English planned to capture and secure this last open entry to the city and then starve the French into surrendering. Morale was low within the town and many of the city's leaders had left thinking the cause was hopeless.

In late February 1429, rumors began to circulate of a virgin savior coming from Lorraine. Pilgrims and peddlers had seen a young maid, dressed as a boy, astride a war-horse and accompanied by a few men-at-arms along the road from Vaucouleurs to Chinon. The rumors spread so quickly that Count Dunois, the city's most passionate defender, sent messengers to Chinon to confirm these travelers' accounts. This person was Joan of Arc.

On May 4, Joan was beginning an afternoon rest when she abruptly walked up her squire. "In God's name, my counsel has told me I must attack the English," she told him. Quickly arming, she called for her horse and rode toward the Burgundy Gate where she saw Frenchmen running back to the city; some wounded.

Dunois had initiated an attack on the English fortresses at St. Loup, approximately two miles east of the city, without notifying Joan. The French were in full retreat when Joan arrived. Seeing her with her white standard raised high, the French soldiers cheered, returned to the assault and fought with such vigor that the English abandoned the attack. One hundred fourteen English were dead and forty were taken prisoner. It was the first time in the seven-month siege that the French had captured an English fortification. Furthermore, had the French lost, the English would have captured the Burgundy Gate sealing off Orléans completely.

Joan's next objective was the Tourelles, a fortification to the south of the Orléans. The attack started at dawn. She did not wear a helmet that day because she wanted to be clearly seen. She was about to step onto a scaling ladder when she was wounded in the neck by an arrow. She was carried to a meadow, where someone cut off the arrow tip. Joan then pulled out the shaft herself. After resting for awhile she returned to the battle.

Darkness was setting in, the towers had not been captured and the troops were exhausted after thirteen hours of battle. Dunois was about to sound retreat. However, Joan persuaded him to wait, let the troops eat and rest, and then renew the attack.

After praying, Joan seized her standard, joined the attack and charged into a ditch below a rampart. "Watch for the moment when the tip of my standard touches the rampart," she told her page. When the page cried, "Joan, the tip is touching!" she shouted, "It's all yours. Go in!"

The French stormed in from all sides. Carpenters had been working feverishly to build a wooden walkway from ladders, boards and gutters to breach the break in the stone bridge leading to the northern walls of the Tourelles. Hoisted into place by ropes and pulleys, French soldiers streamed over the wall. The English panicked when they saw they were being surrounded from both the north and the south. Retreating to a drawbridge the English found the French had set fire to a barge filled with oil soaked rags, pitch, and bundles of sticks under the drawbridge. As the soldiers rushed across the wooden bridge it collapsed. All the soldiers drowned, the weight of their armor dragged them to their death. The seven-month siege of Orléans was over. It had taken only three days of fighting under Joan's inspiration to end it.[11]

There are other historical examples of women distinguishing themselves in combat. The website *gendergap.com* cites these examples:

1. Septima Zenonbia governed Syria from about 250 to 275 AD lead her armies on horseback wearing full armor. During Claudius' reign she defeated the Roman legions so decisively that they retreated from much of Asia Minor. Arabia, Armenia and Persia allied themselves with her and she claimed dominion over Egypt by right of ancestry. Claudius'

successor Aurelian sent his most experienced legions to conquer Zenobia but it took almost 4 years of battles and sieges before her capital city of Palmyra fell. Aurelian later exiled Zenobia to Tibur. Her daughters later married into influential Roman families and her line continued to be important in Roman politics for almost 300 years.

2. Sisters Trung Trae and Trung Nhi led a revolt of Vietnamese peasants against Chinese rule in the first century. Both sisters led their troops in battle and both were noted for their heroism. In 40 A.D. they led an army of 80,000 peasants against To Dihn forcing him to flee to China and freeing Vietnam from Chinese control for the first time in 1,000 years. They controlled 65 fortified cities and trained 36 women, including their mother, as generals. When they were eventually defeated by the numerically superior Chinese reinforcements they committed suicide rather than be captured.

3. Ludmilla Pavichenko, a sniper in the Soviet Army is credited with killing 309 Germans. Lance Corporal Maria Ivanova Morozova served with the 62nd Rifle Battalion and was awarded 11 combat decorations. After the war she became a senior accountant at a factory in Minsk.

4. Elaine Mordeaux was a French Resistance commander during World War II. She led her unit in an attack on the 101st Panzers. Two hundred guerrillas, approximately one third of them women killed more than three thousand Germans in one hour and disabled almost one hundred trucks and tanks. The remaining survivors reported that Ms. Mordeaux continued fighting until a sniper killed her.[12]

More recent examples include CPT Linda Bray actions in Panama during Operation Just Cause in December 1989 when she led thirty soldiers of the 988th Military Police Company to seized an enemy objective near Panama City. Her military objective was to take control of the Panamanian Defense Forces attack dog kennels where defenses were presumed to be light. However, what was supposed to be a routine military police operation turned into a three-hour engagement.

Many critics of women in the military dismiss CPT Linda Bray's actions as "grossly exaggerated." "The sorts of things they were doing [in Panama] could have been done by a 12-year-old with a rifle," jeered Brian Mitchell, author of *Weak Link: The Feminization of the American Military.*[13]

Who do you believe? The initial *New York Times* headline "For the First Time a Woman Leads G.I.'s in Combat" or the *Los Angeles Times* headline "Female's War Exploits overblown, Army Says"?[14]

Other action during Operation Just Cause involved two female pilots, 1LT Lisa Kutschera and Warrant Officer Debra Mann flying two Army Black Hawk helicopters when heir helicopters came under heavy fire during the operation. One had to be grounded after it was hit. A third helicopter was fired on during a supply mission. Three women Army pilots were nominated for the Air Medal and two of them received the "V" for valor.[15]

While women did not serve in direct combat units such as infantry, armor, and cannon artillery, female soldiers in support units often found themselves in the middle of the action. In the Gulf War the front lines were not what they used to be and noncombat units also took casualties. Units in the rear areas were often exposed to attack as those at the front. A Scud missile crashed into the barracks of the 14th Quartermaster Detachment, located in the rear area, killing twenty-eight soldiers, including three women. Iraqi long-range artillery and surface-to-surface missiles did not distinguish between combat and combat support troops.

CPT Cynthia Mosley commanded A Company of the 24th Support Battalion Forward, 24th Infantry Division (Mechanized). The mission of the 100 soldiers of her company was to provide a mechanized brigade with fuel, ammunition, water, and anything else the brigade needed to function in the field. During a ground assault on Highway 8 into Iraq, the company followed closely behind the advancing units. At one point, combat forces were advancing so quickly that they were running out of fuel. As the support unit closest to the front, Alpha Company refueled Bradley fighting vehicles and M1 tanks on the side of the road so they could continue the attack. For a while, the unit was not only supporting they were assigned to, but all the brigades in that area. The Army later awarded CPT Mosley the Bonze Star medal for meritorious combat service.[16]

The debate of the role of women in the military or business will not be resolved soon. In his book, *The Dilbert Future,* Scott Adams predicts women will run the world in all democratic countries. He bases this on two assertions. First, women already control the world. Second, if they don't control the world, who's going to stop them?[17] Adams may have a point.

Conclusions

The previous chapters of this book have shown how businesses incorporate military tactics into their business strategy. Businesses such as Mitsubishi and Miller used fast cycle times to preempt their competition. Miller Brewing Company also used dislocation to produce low volume products more economically. 7UP™ used the disruption technique against Coke™ and Pepsi™ in the 1980s when it introduced its "no caffeine" campaign. Companies can also utilize guerrilla operations to develop niche markets.

In order for an army to succeed, it must coordinate four areas Personnel (S1), Intelligence (S2), Operations (S3), Logistics (S4). Companies must coordinate these same areas. Sales can't sell if they can't deliver a product. Manufacturing can't build a product if it doesn't have the personnel or the correct parts. Logistics can't function if it doesn't know what its going to be receiving or transporting.

One company that utilized the talents of military personnel was General Electric. When its transportation business couldn't find quality people at its Erie, Pennsylvania, headquarters it began recruiting junior military officers. The officers were so successful that other GE units also began recruiting junior officers. When the company had 80, CEO Jack Welch invited them to Farifield where he spent an entire day with them. Impressed with the officers' abilities and accomplishments, Welch required that GE annually hire 200 junior military officers a year. As of 1998, GE had 711 of them on their payroll and many have already achieved notable promotions.

One thing the military and successful companies try to instill is loyalty. However, not only do subordinates have to be loyal to the company but also the company must be loyal to its employees. General George C. Patton realized when he commanded. He wrote:

> Loyalty is frequently only considered as faithfulness from the bottom up.
>
> It has another and equally important application; that is from the top down.
>
> One of the most frequently noted characteristics of the great is unforgetfulness of any loyalty to their subordinates. It is this characteristic which binds, with hoops of iron, their juniors to them.[1]

Yet, many corporations do not want loyalty anymore and this could be setting a dangerous precedent. If a company discards its employees, who's going to lead the company later on? Successful companies such as General Electric, 3M, Nordstrom, Hewlett-Packard and Boeing develop their future management.

Consider Jack Welch of General Electric. Welch joined GE directly out of graduate school and worked for the company twenty consecutive years before becoming chief executive officer. While Welch ranks as one of the most effective chief executive officers in American business, his predecessors were also very capable leaders. Over the course of 100 years, GE executives rank as some of the most effective CEOs in American business history. Reginald Jones, Jack Welch's immediate predecessor, was named in a *U.S. News and World Report* survey of his colleagues to be "the most influential person in business today" in 1979 and 1980. Ralph Cordiner CEO from 1950-1963 restructured and decentralized the company while moving GE into new markets. He was also one the first CEOs to institute the technique management by objective. Cordiner also created Crotonville, GE's management training center and wrote the influential book *New Frontiers for Professional Managers.* Furthermore, more GE alumni have become CEOs at American companies than any other company.[2]

Colonel Ardent du Picq the nineteenth century military theorist wrote "The instruments of battle are valuable only if one knows how to use them." Even if a company has an effective organization, adequate resources, and a suitable product, it still needs to be able to defeat its competition. A study of business history suggests companies such as Xerox, AEG-Telefuken, Braniff, and RCA could have possibly avoided some of their financial losses had they applied the principles of maneuver warfare.

The study of warfare not only teaches one how to win. It also teaches one how not to lose. "Great military commanders are after all, managers most of the time;" write James Dunnigan and Daniel Masterson, authors of *The Way of the Warrior.* "Victory in battle is 90 percent preparation and 10 percent taking care of unanticipated emergencies." Both military and commercial operations must be organized, planned, and executed. It's a point worth remembering before undertaking your next business endeavor.

About the Author

Dave Leppanen is a military intelligence officer in the United States Army Reserve. In the civilian sector he has worked in the areas of administration and logistics.

He currently resides in Mahtomedi, Minnesota.

Notes

Six Similarities between Business and Warfare

1. Seth Lubove, "Get Them Before they Get You, *Forbes,* July 13, 1995, 88.

2. James C. Collins and Jerry I. Porras, *Built To Last, Successful Habits of Visionary Companies* New York: Harper Business, 1994), 115.

3. FM 22-102 *Soldier Team Development* (Washington, DC: Headquarters, Department of the Army, 1987), v.

4. Kenneth Blachard, Ph.D., Donald Carew, Ed.D., Eunice Parisi-Carew, Ed.D., *The One Minute Manager Builds High Performing Teams* (New York: William Morrow and Company, Inc., 1990),

5. James C. Collins and Jerry I. Porras, *Built to Last, Successful Habits of Visionary Companies* (New York: HarperBusiness, 1997), 127.

6. John T. Malloy, *John T. Malloy's New Dress for Success* (New York: Warner Books; 80, 328.

7. Robert Carey, "Winning Ways," *Successful Meetings* October 1993.

8. John A. Bryne, "Requiem for CEO's," *Executive Excellence* April 10, 1993.

9. FM 100-5 *Operations* (Washington, DC: Headquarters, Department of the Army, 1986), 14-18.

10. Sun Tzu, *The Art of War*, Samuel B. Griffith, trans. (Oxford: Oxford University Press, 1963), 77.

11. John G. Meyer, Jr., *Company Command the Bottom Line* Washington, DC: National Defense University Press), 26.

12. William A. Cohen, The *Art of the Leader*, (New Jersey: Prentice Hall, 1990), 6.

13. Carl Von Clausewitz, *On War*, (London: Penguin Books, 1982), 164.

14. Michael Treacy, Fred Wiersema, *The Discipline of Market Leaders*, (Reading, Massachusetts: Addison-Wesley Publishing Company) 29-30.

15. Richard S. Wellins, William C. Byham, George R. Dixon, *Inside Teams*, (San Francisco, Jossey-Bass Publishers); 1, 64.

The Principles of War

1. James C. Collins and Jerry I. Porras, *Built to Last*, (New York, 1994), 128.

2. William C. Symonds and Carol Matlack, "Gillette's Edge," *Business Week*, January 19, 1998, 72.

3. Barrie G. James, *Business Wargames*, (Harmondsworth, Middlesex, England, 1984), 83-84.

4. Lynn Underwood, "Edina Boutique Offers Custom-fit Bras," *Minneapolis Tribune*, August 27, 1998, E3.

5. Collins and Porras, 209.

6. Ibid, 150.

7. Ibid, 161.

8. Ibid, 161-163.

9. John A. Byrne, "How Jack Welch Runs GE," *BusinessWeek*, June 8, 1998.

10. James, 88.

11. James, 88-89.

12. Collins and Porras, 117, 138.

13. Richard Marcinko, *Leadership Secrets of the Rogue Warrior*, (New York, Pocket Books, 1997), 102-104.

Principles of Maneuver Warfare

1. Bevin Alexander, *How Great Generals Win*, (New York, NY: W.W. Norton & Company, 1993), 19-21.

2. Ibid, 124.

3. Ibid, 214, 219

4. Omar Bradley and Clay Blair, *A General's Life: An autobiography* (New York: Simon & Schuster, 1983), 544.

5. Robert Leonhard, *The Art of Maneuver*, (Novato CA: Presido Press, 1991), 79-80.

6. Ibid., 68-72.

7. J.N. Westwood, *The History of the Middle East Wars*, New York: Exter Boois-), 85-87.

8. Joseph J. Romm, "The Gospel According to Sun Tzu", *Forbes* December 9, 1991: 156.

9. Ibid, 161-162.

10. Patricia Sellers, "A Whole New Ballgame in Beer." *Fortune* 19 Sept. 1994, 84.

11. Leonhard, 66-67.

12. Ibid, 68-73.

13. Sellers, 84-86.

14. George Beran, "Dry Idea For Homes." *St. Paul Pioneer Press*, 20 Aug. 1995: 6D.

15. Leonard, 13.

16. B.H. Liddell Hart, *History of the Second World War*, (Pedigree Books, New York, 1982), 66-68.

17. 16. Ibid, 68-71.

18. Robert L. Pfaltzgraff, Jr. and Richard H. Shultz, Jr. *The United States Army Challenges and Missions for the 1990s*, (Lexington Books, Lexington, Massachusetts, 1991), 78.

19. Al Ries and Jack Trout, *Marketing Warfare*, New American Library, New York, 1986), 145

20. Tom Peters, *Liberation Management Necessary Disorganization for the Nanosecond Nineties,* Alfred A. Knopf, New York, 1992), 32-38.

21. FM 71-3, *Armored and Mechanized Infantry Brigade,* (Washington, D.C.), Headquarters, Department of the Army), 3-10.

22, Ries and Trout, 145.

23. Garfield, Bob. "Liet goes smug, hip, but results fall flat." *Advertising Age* Feb 3, 1997. http://www.adage.com/news_and_features/ad_review/archives/ar19970203.html

24. Collins and Porras, 82.

25. 82-83.

Guerrilla Operations

1. Bevin Alexander, *The Future of Warfare,* (W.W. Norton & Company, Inc., New York, 1995), 131

2. Ibid, 46-47

3. Samuel B. Griffith II, *Mao Tse-Tung on Guerrilla Warfare,* (The Nautical & Aviation Publishing Company of America, Baltimore, Maryland, 1992), 35-36.

4. Alexander, 162-163.

5. Ries and Trout, 116.

6. Paul Levy, "She Gives a Weather Wakeup Call to Cities," *Minneapolis Star Tribune* 15 Jan. 1997: E1.

Staff Operations

1. FM 101-5 *Staff Organization and Operations,* (Washington, DC: Headquarters, Department of the Army, 1997), 4-9 to 4-10.

2. Wendy Zeller, "Go-Go Goliaths," *Business Week* 13 February, 1995: 69.

3. Dick Youngblood, "Corporate Judo Helps Smaller Firms," *Minneapolis Tribune,* June 10, 1996: D2.

4. Lisa Harden, "Non-Traditional Workforce Becomes Valuable Resource In Tight Labor Market," *Minnesota Business Ink*, September-October 1997, 20.

5. B.H. Liddell Hart, *History of the Second World War*, (New York: Putnam, 1971F, 350.

6. Ibid., 153.

7. FM 101-5, *Staff Organization and Operations*, (Washington, DC: Headquarters, Department of the Army, 1984), 4-10 to 4-11.

8. James A. Belasco and Ralph C.Stayer, *Flight of the Buffalo*, (New York: Warner, 1993), 159.

9. Harvey Mackay, *Swim with the Sharks without Being Eaten Alive*, (New York, Ballatine Books, 1988), 223-230.

10. Ronald E. Yate, "Espionage Fight Shifts to Corporate Battlefield," *Chicago Tribune*, 24 March 1996.

11. Ibid..

12. Al Ries and Jack Trout, *Marketing Warfare* (New York: New American Library, 1986), 61.

13. Ibid, 62

14. Department of the Army, Washington, DC: Headquarters. *Field Manual (FM) 101-5 Staff Organization and Operations*, 1984, 4-12 to 4-14.

15. James F. Dunnigan and Austin Bay, *From Shield to Storm* (New York: William Morrow and Company, Inc.), 263-265.

16. Ibid., 272-276.

17. Ibid., 277-279.

18. Ibid., 278-282.

19. Wendy Zeller et al. "Go Go Goliaths," *Business Week*, February 13, 1995, 70.

20. David Kirpatrick, The Second Coming of Apple, *Fortune*, November 9, 1998.

21. Robert D. Hof, Ira Sger, Linda Himelstein, *The Sad Saga of Silicon Graphics*, *Business Week*, August 4, 1997, 66.

22. Ibid, 68, 70.

23. FM 101-5 *Staff Organization and Operations*, (Washington, DC: Headquarters, Department of the Army, 1997), H-12, H-13.

24. Dunnigan and Bay, *From Shield to Storm*, 151.

25. Ibid.

26. FM 101-5 Staff *Organization and Operations* (Washington DC: Headquarters, Department of the Army), 3-9, 3-0.

27. David F. Bond, "Troop and Materiel Deployment Missions Central Elements in Desert Storm Success," *Aviation Week & Space Technology*, April 22, 1991: 92. Dunnigan and Bay 238-242.

28. Russell Mitchell and Seth Payne, "Half Audie Murphy, Half Jack Welch," *Business Week*, March 4, 1991: 42.

29. Ronald Henkoff, "Delivering the Goods," *Fortune* November 28, 1993: 64.

30. Ibid, 76-78.

31. Michael Treacy and Fred Wiersema, *The Discipline of Market Leaders*, (Reading, Massachusetts: Addison-Wesley Publishing, 1994), 53.

32. Ibid, 32-34.

Deception

1. Dunnigan, James F., and Albert A. Nofi *Victory and Deceit Dirty Tricks of* War. New York: William Morrow and Company, 1995), 29-30.

2. Ibid, 10-13.

3. Dunnigan, James F., and Austin Bay *From Shield to Storm.*(New York: William Morrow and Company, 1992),

4. Ibid, 266-67.

5. Robert Leonard, *The Art of Maneuver*, (Novato: Presido Press, 1991), 265.

6. Chin-Ning Chu, *Thick Face, Black Heart*, (New York: Time Warner, 1992), 185-188.

7. Robert A.Melcher and Sandra Dallas, "From the Microbrewers Who Brought You Bud, Coors..." *Business Week*, April 24, 1995, p. 66, 70.

Leadership

1. SSG David Abrams, "MSG (Ret) Roy Benavidez, A Real American Hero," *The NCO Journal*, Spring 1996.

2. FM 22-100, *Army Leadership*, (Washington DC: Headquarters, Department of the Army, 1999), 1-4.

3. Stuart R. Levine and Michael A. Crom, The Leader in You, (Simon & Schuster, New York), p. 21.

4. William A. Cohen, *The Art of the Leader*, (Prentice Hall, New Jersey: 1990), 9

5. Washington DC: American Forces Information Service Department of Defense DoD GEN-36, *The Armed Forces Officer* (1975), 22.

6. Hyrum W. Smith, *The 10 Natural Laws of Successful Time and Life Management*, (Warner Books: New York, 1994), 205-207.

7. Tom Peters, *Liberation Management Necessary Disorganization for the Nanosecond Nineties*, (Alfred A. Knopf: New York, 1992), 99-100.

8. Cohen, 6

9. Ibid, 17.

10. James C. Collins and Jerry I. Porras, *Built to Last, Successful Habits of Visionary Companies*, HarperCollins, New York, 1994), 147.

11. Ibid, 141.

12. Ibid, 141.

13. Cohen, 7-8.

14. James A. Belasco and Ralph C.Stayer, *Flight of the Buffalo* (New York: Warner, 1993), 139-140.

15. Collins and Porras, 118-119.

16. Cohen, 26.

17. Dan Carrison and Rod Walsh, *Semper Fi Leadership the Marine Corps Way*, (New York, American Management Association, 1998), 212-214.

18. Harvey Mackay, *Swim with the Sharks without Being Eaten Alive*, (New York, Ballatine Books, 1988), 138-139.

19. Meyer, John G., *Company Command the Bottom Line*, (National Defense University Press, Washington D.C., 1990), 165.

20. Tom Peters, *Liberation Management Necessary Disorganization for the Nanosecond Nineties*, (Alfred A. Knopf: New York, 1992), 89-90.

Training

1. Meyer, John G., *Company Command the Bottom Line*, (National Defense University Press, Washington D.C., 1990), 120.

2. FM 101-5 *Staff Organizations and Operations* (Washington, DC: Headquarters, Department of the Army, 31 May 1997), 4-12.

3. Joesph J. Romm, "The Gospel According to Sun Tzu", *Forbes*, December 9, 1991, p. 160.

4. Clay Carr, *Smart Training, The Manager's Guide to Training for Improved Performance* (McGraw-Hillm Inc. New York, 1992), 18-21.

5. Wendy Zeller et al. "Go Go Goliaths," *Business Week*, February 13, 1995, 69

6. Dan Carrison and Rod Walsh, *Semper Fi, Business Leadership the Marine Corps Way* (American Management Association, New York, 1998), 37.

7. James C. Collins and Jerry I. Porras, *Built to Last Successful Habits of Visionary Companies*, (HarperCollins, New York, 1997), 127.

8. John Bryne, "The Search for the Young and Gifted," *Business Week*, October 4, 1999, p. 116.

9. Carrison and Walsh, 139.

Women in the Workplace and the Military

1. Fact Sheet Labor Day 1998, www.catalystwomen.org/press/factlabor.html.

2. Associated Press, "Women Gaining in Pay Disparity with Men," *Minneapolis StarTribune*, June 10, 1998: D1.

3. Associated Press, "Women Mean Business," *Minneapolis StarTribune,* April 28, 1999: D1.

4. Diane E. Lewis, "More Women are Becoming Family's Primary Breadwinner," *Minneapolis StarTribune,* June 10,1998: D2

5. Sarah Craciunolu, "A Rising Star," *Soldiers,* July 1997, 26.

6. "New General is an Army First," ARNEWS, June 2, 1997.

7. Lt. Col. Randy Pullen, "Army Reserve Gets its First Woman 2-Star General," *Army Reserve,* Vol. 45, Number 2, p. 8.

8. Mary Leonard, "Report is Grist for Foes of Coed Military Training, NewsBank, Inc. *Star Tribune,* December 28, 1997, p. 2.

9. Ibid, 2.

10. Elisabetta Addis et. Al, *Women Soldiers Images Realities,* (New York: St. Martins Press, 1994), 64.

11. Polly Schoyer Brooks, *Beyond the Myth, The Story of Joan of Arc,* New York: Harper Collins 3. Publishers, 1990), 55-67.

12. "Women Warriors," www.gendergap.com

13. Linda Bird Francke, *Ground zero: the Gender Wars in the Military,* (New York: Simon and Schuster, 1997), 56.

14. Ibid, 59-60.

15. Jeanne Holm, *Women in the Military: an Unfinished Revolution,* (Novato, CA: Presido Press, 1993), 435.

16. Ibid, 452.

17. Scott Adams, *Dilbert Future,* (New York: HarperBusiness, 1997), 108.

Conclusions

1. Walter J. Ridge, *Follow Me! Business Leadership Patton Style,* New York: American Management Association, 1989), 45.

2. Collins and Porras, 170-173.

Bibliography

Addis, Elisabetta et al., *Women Soldiers Images and Realities* (New York, St. Martin's Press), 1994.

Alexander, Bevin. *The Future of Warfare,* (New York, W.W. Norton & Company), 1995.

Alexander, Bevin. *How Great Generals Win,* (New York, W.W. Norton & Company), 1993.

American Forces Information Service Department of Defense, *DoD* Washington, DC: *GEN-36, The Armed Forces Officer),* 1975.

James A. Belasco and Ralph C.Stayer, *Flight of the Buffalo* (New York: Warner, 1993).

Blachard, Kenneth Ph.D., Carew, Donald Ed.D., Parisi-Carew, EuniceEd.D. *The One Minute Manager Builds High Performing Teams* (New York: William Morrow and Company, Inc., 1990)

David F. Bond, "Troop and Materiel Deployment Missions Central Elements in Desert Storm Success," *Aviation Week & Space Technology,* April 22, 1991: 92.

Beran, George. "Dry Idea For Homes." *St. Paul Pioneer Press,* 20 Aug. 1995: 6D.

Bryne, John A. "Requiem for CEO's," *Executive Excellence* April 10, 1993.

Carey, Robert ."Winning Ways," *Successful Meetings* October 1993.

Carrison, Dan and Rod Walsh, *Semper Fi Leadership the Marine Corps Way,* (New York: American Management Association, 1998).

Chu, Chin-Ning. *Thick Face, Black Heart,* (New York: Time Warner, 1992).

Clausewitz, Carl Von. *On War,* (London, England: Penguin Books, Ltd), 1968.

Cohen, William A. The *Art of the Leader,* (New Jersey: Prentice Hall, 1990).

Collins, James C. and Porras, Jerry I. *Built to Last, Successful Habits of Visionary Companies* (New York: HarperBusiness, 1997).

Department of the Army, (Washington, DC: Headquarters. *Field Manual FM 22-100 Army Leadership,* 1999).

Department of the Army, (Washington, DC: Headquarters. *Field Manual 100-5 Operations,* 1993).

Department of the Army, (Washington, DC: Headquarters. *Field Manual 101-5 Staff Organization and Operations,*1984).

Department of the Army, Washington, DC: Headquarters. *Field Manual 22-102 Soldier Team Development* (1987).

Dunnigan, James F., and Albert A. Nofi *Victory and Deceit Dirty Tricks of* War. (New York: William Morrow and Company, 1995).

Dunnigan, James F. and Austin Bay, *From Shield to Storm* (New York: William Morrow and Company, Inc. 1992).

Hart, B.H. Liddell. *History of the Second World War,* (Pedigree Books, New York, 1982).

Henkoff, Ronald. "Delivering the Goods," *Fortune* November 28, 1993: 64.

Leonhard, Robert. *The Art of Maneuver,* (Novato CA: Presido Press, 1991).

Levine, Stuart R. and Crom, Michael A. *The Leader in You,* (Simon & Schuster, New York), p. 21.

Levy, Paul. "She Gives a Weather Wakeup Call to Cities," *Minneapolis Star Tribune* 15 Jan. 1997:

Malloy, John T. *John T. Malloy's New Dress for Success* (New York: Warner Books, 1997).

Melcher, Robert A. and Dallas, Sandra. "From the Microbrewers Who Brought You Bud, Coors..." *Business Week,* April 24, 1995, p. 66, 70.

Meyer, John G. Jr. *Company Command the Bottom Line* Washington, DC: National Defense University Press), 26.

Mitchell, Russell and Payne, Seth. "Half Audie Murphy, Half Jack Welch," *Business Week,* March 4, 1991: 42.

Tom Peters, *Liberation Management Necessary Disorganization for the Nanosecond Nineties,* Alfred A. Knopf, New York, 1992).

Pfaltzgraff, Robert L. Jr. and Shultz, Richard H. Jr. *The United States Army Challenges and Missions for the 1990s,* (Lexington Books, Lexington, Massachusetts, 1991).

Ries, Al and Trout, Jack. *Marketing Warfare* (New York: New American Library, 1986).

Romm, Joseph J. "The Gospel According to Sun Tzu", *Forbes* December 9, 1991: 156.

Sellers, Patricia. "A Whole New Ballgame in Beer." *Fortune* 19 Sept. 1994, 86.

Sun Tzu, *The Art of War,* Samuel B. Griffith, trans. (Oxford: Oxford University Press, 1963).

Treacy, Michael and Wiersema, Fred. *The Discipline of Market Leaders,* (Reading, Massachusetts: Addison Wesley Publishing, 1994).

Westwood, J.N. *The History of the Middle East Wars,* New York: Exter Boois), 85-87.

Yate, Ronald E., "Espionage Fight Shifts to Corporate Battlefield," *Chicago Tribune,* 24 March 1996.

Youngblood, Dick "Corporate Judo Helps Smaller Firms," *Minneapolis Tribune,* 10 June 1996: D2.

Index

Principles of war
Gen Carl von
Clausewitz

" Pursue one great decisive aim
   with force & determination"

" A General, who with tyrannical authority
   demands of his troops the most extreme
   exertions & the greatest privations, ... "

"... For the aim of historians rarely is to
   present the absolute truth. Usually they
   wish to embellish the deeds..."

" A powerful emotion must stimulate
   the great ability of a military leader,
   wether it be ambition as in Caesar,
   hatred of the enemy as in Hannibal,
   or the pride in a glorious defeat, as
   in Frederick the Great.♣

      Open your heart to such emotion.
      Be audacious & cunning in your plans.

"... We can triumph over such obstacles
only with very great exertion, & to accomplish
this the leader must show a severity bordering
on cruelty."
                    of many!
 ♣ The origins of fascism!
                    MDC

Jan 20, 2011

9 780595 141081